RHODODENDRONS

WITH

CAMELLIAS and MAGNOLIAS
2006

GW00370479

Royal
Horticultural
Society

Published in 2006 by
The Royal Horticultural Society,
80 Vincent Square, London SW1P 2PE

ISBN 1 902896 59 9

Edited for the RHS by Simon Maughan

Honorary Editor for the Rhododendron, Camellia and Magnolia Group
Philip Evans

Editorial Subcommittee
Maurice Foster
Rosemary Foster
Brian Wright

Honorary Production Manager for the Rhododendron, Camellia and Magnolia Group
Pam Hayward

Opinions expressed by the authors are not necessarily those of
the Royal Horticultural Society

Printed by MPG Books Ltd, Bodmin, Cornwall

COVER ILLUSTRATIONS
FRONT COVER: *Camellia* 'Leonard Messel' (*C. reticulata* × *C. williamsii* 'Mary Christian')
at the Main Camellia Show, Westminster, 12 April 2005 (Michael Shuttleworth)
BACK COVER: *Rhododendron coriaceum* shown by Brian Wright at the Main Rhododendron
Show, Borde Hill, 23 April 2005 (Mike Robinson)
BACK COVER: *Magnolia delavayi* pink form at Kunming, southwest China (Maurice Foster)

CONTENTS

CHAIRMAN'S FOREWORD

MICHAEL ROBINSON

" … the lazy seeds of servile imitation thrown away, and fresh invention planted."
(Thomas Carew c.1595 – 1640)

It was a delight to see a rhododendron stand at Chelsea after so many fallow years: David Millais is to be complimented on his efforts to make the genus popular once more and on the sheer quality of his plants. It was also nice to see more interesting new plants than is usual at Chelsea, though as ever woody plants were under-represented, and I noticed no camellias or magnolias. These are noticeable by their almost complete absence at all the big RHS shows. Why is this? Of course the timing of Hampton Court and Tatton does not help (though nurserymen force other genera to flower out of season), and magnolia blooms hate travel, only looking their superb best when exhibited locally, as in Cornwall or at Borde Hill. Nevertheless, if there were the will (and the market), I believe these difficulties would be overcome.

Perhaps it is the concept of a rhododendron or camellia garden in the minds of designers and nurserymen that is the problem. Their impressions are most likely to be taken from the great collections of rhododendrons and camellias planted in the last century in places where, perhaps, the instinct for the acquisition of 'the complete set' of a genus was within the reach of the owner. Of course, such collections are of great importance historically and ecologically, and their present decline into incompleteness will concern many in the Group, but that is another matter. However, it has to be admitted that they can be dull viewing out of season, and it may be that the impression that a rhododendron garden (in particular) is one with little but rhododendrons in it that is responsible for the lack of popularity of the genus. Similarly, a garden with little in it but camellias would be repetitive indeed for many months of the year. Collections of magnolias (and there continue to be many excellent new hybrids each year) are more recent, and it is noticeable that these are much more varied, with many other genera interspersed.

The appearance in the yearbook of articles on companion plants and on extending the season has begun to address this problem, but perhaps we need to publicise more the contribution that combinations of <u>woody</u> plants can make to effective and lasting garden design.

Foliage is the key to this – a plant must pull its weight for twelve months, no matter how spectacular its flowers may be, but our genera offer more chances of striking foliage combinations than do many others. Many will occur to readers, but here are a few examples:

A startling tropical effect is created by planting *Magnolia dealbata* with a big-leaved rhododendron and *Camellia* 'Francie L' with its strange leaves: the flowers – (and what flowers!) are a bonus here. By all means sling in a banana and underplant with cannas, hedychiums, and roscoeas to complete the structure, plus a few black-leaved ophiopogons, but forget the tree fern for once.

The combination of the silver-leaved *Rhododendron pachysanthum* 'Crosswater form' with *R. physocarpus* 'Diablo' is stunning. The dark-red-leaved rhododendrons being developed at Glendoick allow the reverse effect – they would look stunning with a silver-leaved plant such as *Artemisia* 'Valerie Finnis'. A shiny leaved camellia in brightest green would complete the picture.

The glaucous leaves of *Rhododendron cinnabarinum, R. oreotrephes* and the best forms of *R. caloxanthum,* are wonderful with pink roses.

The autumn colour of many azaleas can be set to act as a foil to maples and *Rosa glauca* in fruit.

As Maurice Foster does so successfully, varieties of *Clematis viticella* can be grown through magnolias – these climbers can be cut to the ground each February and do not interfere with the magnolia display. Incidentally, the underplanting of magnolias with chionodoxas, as Rod Wild does, is entrancing.

I am sure members have many interesting and fabulous plant combinations to share with others, so let us lead fashion rather than follow it.

In this yearbook the theme of companion planting continues, there is more on new and old species and hybrids, a scholarly summary of the developments in magnolia taxonomy, and the article on the emergence of this Group will contain much that is new to all of us. Once again, Philip Evans has produced a fascinating Yearbook, which will enthuse, enlighten, entertain and instruct.

EDITORIAL

PHILIP EVANS

A year or two ago John Gallagher lent me a photo of the late Professor Waterhouse and T. Hope Findlay together – taken (I think) at the Savill Garden – and remarked that Hope Findlay was the finest gardener he had ever met. It is a happy coincidence that in this edition of the Yearbook we learn from two different authors something of Hope Findlay's accomplishments. Mark Flanagan gives an account of his rhododendron hybrids, and also reflects on his wider gardening achievements, whilst Brian Wright reminds us of his introduction of the first UK collection of Kunming Reticulata Camellias at Windsor, and refers to his contribution to the Yearbook in 1964 – a short piece on the cultivation of this spectacular group.

Denny Pratt is another gardener whose hybrid rhododendrons – this time late flowering deciduous azaleas – are not well known commercially. Pratt contributed more than once to the Yearbook about his breeding programme, and it is valuable now to have from Peter Cunnington, a summary, together with a survey of the surviving collection at Ness Garden, of what are now styled the Ness Holt Hybrids. We are fortunate to be able to illustrate one or two of the plants with Joan Wilkinson's delightful watercolours.

There are no less than three excellent magnolia articles in this edition. I would describe Maurice Foster's on 'Summer Flowering Magnolias' as 'definitive'. Dick Figlar was asked to answer, under 'Taxonomy Topics' section, the Editor's naive question – 'Why have michelias now become magnolias?' and, in so doing, he has produced an absolutely comprehensive summary of the current classification of the family magnoliaceae. We also welcome a contribution from Rhoda Maurer and Eric Hsu of the Scott Arboretum in Philadelphia about the collection there.

I am glad that our occasional series on companion planting continues, with an expert contribution on hydrangeas from Shelagh Newman – custodian of the National Collection at Holebird and also the new Chairman of the Lakeland Rhododendron Society. Reverting to rhododendrons there is a helpful article from Gerald Dixon on the hybrids of the late Hans Robenek, a German breeder possibly little known in the UK.

As a diversion, we can all, from the comfort of our armchairs, return with Peter and Patricia Cox and their party to the Indian Himalaya of Arunachal Pradesh, and the rhododendron species and primulas along the Bhutan border.

Finally, David Farnes, who retired in 2005, one of the longest serving members of the Executive Committee, has, at the Chairman's request, recorded a personal memoir of the evolution of the Group to its present form.

THOMAS HOPE FINDLAY
AND HIS RHODODENDRONS

MARK FLANAGAN

Thomas Hope Findlay was born in the estate bothy at Logan, near Stranraer, on 21 April 1910. As the son of a head gardener, Hope was brought up in that tradition of great Scottish gardeners, which emphasised hard work, application and attention to detail. To these virtues Hope added his own flair and the imagination that is so evident in the plantings in the Savill and Valley Gardens and was celebrated in his Chelsea show gardens during the middle decades of the 20th century.

Robert Findlay took his family south prior to the First World War eventually becoming curator of Wisley. Hope followed the same path into private service when he took up employment at Pyrford Court near Woking in Surrey, the seat of Lord Iveagh.

By the time he reached his early thirties he was Head Gardener to Sir James Horlick at Little Paddocks, part of the Titness Park estate near Sunningdale, whose garden, on that great seam of Bagshot sand which wends its way through north-west Surrey and adjacent parts of Berkshire, was celebrated for its woodland gems. It was from Little Paddocks that Hope was 'head-hunted' by Sir Eric Savill, commencing his employment in Windsor Great Park on 1 January 1943.

At that time the Savill Garden was barely ten years in the making and already suffering from the exigencies of wartime neglect; the Valley Gardens were, at most, just an idea in Sir Eric's mind. Hope threw himself into his new position with characteristic vigour and enthusiasm. In Sir Eric he had a hard taskmaster but a man of vision and authority. Over nearly thirty years, until Savill's retirement in 1970, they jointly created the finest woodland gardens in the

MARGARET FINDLAY

Thomas Hope Findlay

country, in the words of that noted horticultural commentator, Arthur Hellyer:

> *'Between them the Savill and Valley Gardens provide an object lesson in all that is best in 20th century garden making.'*

It was said that Eric Savill could look at a wilderness and see a garden, and though Savill set out the bones of the landscape, it was Hope who added the flesh. He drew from an encyclopaedic knowledge of hardy plants and was equally at home in the propagation house as he was in the garden. Today the Savill and Valley Gardens have reached maturity and we can appreciate Hope's genius. Delightful vignettes are everywhere – from the exhilarating sweep of the Azalea Valley to the intimacy of the peat beds in the Savill Garden. In every case Hope utilised his in-depth knowledge of the local microclimates and the inherent potential of the landscape to execute a brilliant series of garden areas.

Now, some 10 years after his death, Hope is remembered by few; his contemporaries are gone and the succeeding generations found new horticultural heroes. Even less well-known is Hope's skill as a breeder, principally of rhododendrons but also of daffodils and other plants. Posterity has not been kind to his rhododendron hybrids. They were bred to grace the great woodland gardens of the British Isles at a time when such gardens were beginning to wane. His use of new species and novel combinations didn't always produce the expected results and the resultant progeny were never distributed extensively enough to gain widespread approbation. But, despite this, his imagination and thoroughness have left us some lovely plants that still deserve to be better known.

MARK FLANAGAN

Rhododendron 'Crowthorne' (*R. souliei* FCC x *aberconwayi*)

It is likely that Hope was involved with the Horlick Hybrids, so it is not surprising that his breeding programme at Windsor began within a year of his arrival and continued until 1968. During this period he made 288 separate crosses of which 56 were named. Unfortunately we have no in-depth written records of this programme and much of what follows is the result of personal observation, analysis of the results of Hope's work and, all too brief, conversations with the late John Bond.

It would seem that initially flower colour was his guiding principle, much as it had informed the breeding work at Exbury and Bodnant. Between 1944 and 1947 the majority of plants raised had pink flowers – for instance 'Bray' and 'Seven Stars'. This was followed by a red period during the years 1948 to 1951 – 'Appleford' and 'Red Rum'. With yellows (a favourite colour of Sir Eric Savill) dominating during the early 1950s – 'Binfield' and 'Theale' for example. After this point the crosses become much more diverse

and many of Hope's loveliest hybrids date from the mid to late 1950s.

As the programme developed it would seem that Hope had a series of favourite hybrids and species that he used as parents again and again. The Windsor FCC form of *Rhododendron souliei* was used many times as was *R. aberconwayi*, its characteristic saucer-shaped corolla producing several distinctive clones. Of the hybrids, the Exbury pair of 'Hawk' and the various 'Jalisco' clones were repeatedly used. Hope also demonstrated great foresight; in 1947 he was one of the first hybridists to use *R. yakushimanum*, little more than 10 years after its first introduction and his dwarf hybrid 'Chink', itself dating from 1947, anticipated the modern trend towards plants of lesser stature.

Naming hybrids can be tricky, many obvious names will already have been used and so many are saddled with ghastly names. If a breeding programme is underway it can be valuable to adopt a theme as a means to link the plants together. In Hope's case the majority of his hybrids were named after Berkshire towns and villages or areas of the Windsor estate.

Initially, the newly raised plants were held in nursery rows, but as they came into flower they were assessed and if they passed muster were named and planted in the gardens. Over time

MARK FLANAGAN

Rhododendron 'Ardington'
(*R. yakushimanum* x
['Hawk' x *brachycarpum*])

many were shown to the Rhododendron and Camellia Committee, where they found an appreciative audience, gaining many awards. Most were awarded from the vase and judged solely on their flowers. Time has shown us that not all are worthy of esteem but many are and having observed these hybrids closely since 1997, I would like to offer my top 5. I have to confess to having a soft spot for the paler shades which provide such subtlety in the woodland garden, rather than the more stolid oranges and reds. I am also drawn to the primary hybrids, with their inherent sophistication, in preference to the more highly bred multiple crosses.

'Crowthorne' (*souliei* FCC × *aberconwayi*) – a lovely plant from a cross made in 1951 (see picture, page 9). It combines two very distinct species and draws the best attributes from each. The flowers are shell-pink in bud and pass to pure white on opening. The plant stays relatively compact and is very floriferous. It has none of the miffiness of *souliei* nor the rather ordinary foliage of *aberconwayi*.

'Ardington' (*yakushimanum* × ['Hawk' × *brachycarpum*]) – a more complex cross and not an obvious one (see picture, left). Many regard *brachycarpum* as an undistinguished plant, hardy but lacking in refinement. In this hybrid *brachycarpum* is much to the fore and adds greatly to its beauty.

Rhododendron 'Blewbury' (R. roxieanum R59218 × anwheiense)

It has rich pink flowers which have an ethereal quality in the reduced light of the spring woodland. From *yakushimanum* it draws a more interesting leaf and despite the presence of *fortunei* it doesn't make an overlarge specimen.

'Blewbury' (*roxieanum* × *anwheiense*) – perhaps Hope's best known hybrid (see picture, below). This plant is well represented in gardens in the British Isles and can be seen growing in many gardens on the Pacific coast of North America. It is a very distinct plant with narrow leaves forming a dense shrub. The flower trusses are small but neatly formed and well displayed above the foliage, which forms a supporting ruff – like an Elizabethan collar. Its parentage confers a tolerance of more open conditions and the best plants at Windsor are on the woodland edge rather than in the more sheltered interior conditions enjoyed by some of its peers.

'Swallowfield' (*souliei* × *yakushimanum*) – another unlikely cross. Rather than build on the compact habit of *yakushimanum*, Hope

MARK FLANAGAN

Hope Findlay Hybrids

Name	Parentage	WGP Stud No.	Award
'Peregrine'	*souliei* (white form) × 'Hawk'	3/45	PC
'Bray'	Unnamed *griffithianum* hybrid × 'Hawk'	5/46	AM
'Candy Floss'	'Hawk' × 'Mrs Randall Davidson'	12/47	AM
'Swallowfield'	*souliei* × *yakushimanum*	23/47	HC
'Seven Stars'	× *loderi* 'Sir Joseph Hooker' × *yakushimanum*	30/47	FCC
'Chink'	*trichocladum* × *keiskei*	31/47	AM
'Winkfield'	'Jalisco Elect' × 'Fusilier'	32/48	AM
'Easter Bonnet'	× *loderi* × (*ponticum* × *loderi*)	40/48	
'Grilse'	'Jalisco Eclipse' × 'Fusilier'	44/48	AM
'Donnington'	*haematodes* subsp. *chaetomallum* × 'Portia'	47/48	PC
'Appleford'	'Portia' × *barbatum*	48/48	AM
'Brookside'	*griersonianum* × 'Jalisco Goshawk'	51/48	AM
'Cranbourne'	'Isabella' × 'Azor'	55/48/1	AM
'Cranbourne's Sister'	'Isabella' × 'Azor'	55/48/2	
'Silkcap'	*leucaspis* × 'Cilpinense'	57/48	
'Brightwell'	*forrestii* Repens Group (KW 6832) × *barbatum*	60/49	AM
'Lambourn'	'Lady Chamberlain' × *maddenii*	63/49	PC
'Margaret Findlay'	*wardii* × *griersonianum*	73/49	
'Mortimer'	'Gladys' × 'Yvonne Pearl'	76/79	AM
'Red Rum'	'Barclayi' × *forrestii* Repens Group	77a/49	AM
'Tan Crossing'	'Jalisco Goshawk' × 'Jalisco Eclipse'	91/50	AM
'Crowthorne'	*souliei* FCC form × *aberconwayi*	103/51	HC
'Queens Wood'	*souliei* × *aberconwayi*	104/51	AM
'Hope Findlay'	'Creeping Jenny' × (× *loderi* × 'Earl of Athlone')	109/51	AM
'Thicket'	*seinghkuense* × *moupinense*	129/53	PC
'Binfield'	'China' × 'Crest'	130/53	AM
'Theale'	'Penjerrick' × 'Crest'	131/53	AM
'Warfield'	'Jalisco' × 'Crest'	132/53/1	AM
'Buttersteep'	'Jalisco' × 'Crest'	132/53/2	AM
'Bishopsgate'	'Jalisco' × 'Crest'	132/53/3	PC
'Arborfield'	× *loderi* 'Julie' × 'Crest'	134/53	AM
'Clewer'	*wardii* Litiense Group × 'Crest'	136/53	PC
'Queen Elizabeth II'	'Idealist' × 'Crest'	137/53/1	FCC
'Lady in Waiting'	'Idealist' × 'Crest'	137/53/2	AM
'Mah Jong'	'Chink' × *valentinianum*	146/53	PC
'Woodside'	'Halcyone' × *aberconwayi*	156/54/1	PC
'The Queen Mother'	'Halcyone' × *aberconwayi*	156/54/2	AM
'Tilehurst'	'Dido' × 'Sarita Loder'	165/55	PC
'Wantage'	'Fabia' × 'Dido'	170/55	PC
'Fernhill'	'Peregrine' × *yakushimanum*	178/56	AM
'Ardington'	*yakushimanum* × ('Hawk' × *brachycarpum*)	181/56	
'Wishmoor'	*yakushimanum* × *wardii* Litiense Group	182/56	AM
'Kings Ride'	*insigne* × *yakushimanum*	186/56	HC
'Blewbury'	*roxieanum* R59218 × *anwheiense*	188/56	FCC
'Enborne'	*aberconwayi* × *anwheiense*	192/56	AM
'Streatley'	*aberconwayi* × *yakushimanum*	193/56	AM
'Winter Snow'	*chrysodoron* × *moupinense*	198/57	
'Snow Hill'	Wadae Group × *mucronatum*	207/57/1	AM
'Chalk Hill'	Wadae Group × *mucronatum*	207/57/2	AM
'Manor Hill'	'Dido' × ('Jalisco' × *yakushimanum*)	217/58	AM
'Dukeshill'	'Kiev' × Lady Digby	223/61	AM
'Bucklebury'	'Kiev' × *yakushimanum*	224/61	AM
'Englemere'	'Jutland' × 'Royal Blood'	255/61/1	AM
'Royal Windsor'	'Jutland' × 'Royal Blood'	255/61/2	AM
'Whitmoor'	'Grenadine' × 'Royal Blood'	258/65	FCC
'Windlebrook'	*carolinianum* 'Album' × 'Cilpinense'	270/66	PC

Rhododendron 'Clewer'
(*R. wardii* Litiense Group
× 'Crest')

MARK FLANAGAN

seems to have wanted to add the wonderful foliage of this taxon to the flowers and form of *souliei*. The results are quite extraordinary. It is difficult to see much of *yakushimanum* in the progeny. The leaves lack indumentum, are ovate-elliptic and the plant forms an open, airy shrub. Nonetheless the combination is enchanting. The pink, campanulate flowers cascade forward and are produced in loose trusses. A group of plants, from this cross, on the edge of the peat beds in the Savill Gardens never fails to delight in the week leading up to Chelsea.

'Clewer' (*wardii* Litiense Group × 'Crest') – to my mind the best of Hope's many yellows (see picture, above), which to a greater or lesser degree are prone to mildew. Despite this, I admire the beautiful richness of the flowers of this plant which have gorgeous peachy tips when they emerge from the bud. It is perhaps the least gawky of his yellow hybrids and keeps a reasonable shape and coverage as it ages (would that we all could!).

Of the remaining 51 clones, many never made it beyond the woodlands of the Savill and Valley Gardens. I presume Hope himself recognised the decline in both the overall popularity of rhododendrons and in the large woodland hybrids in particular. He restricted his distribution to interested friends and colleagues most of whom had the opportunity to give these plants the conditions that would

do them justice. Today they can be seen in discerning collections, notably in Ray Wood at Castle Howard, thanks to the taste and industry of James Russell, and on Battleston Hill at Wisley. For the record I have included a list of the Hope Findlay hybrids of which we have some records, though readers should realise that, with a few exceptions, these are only those he bred using members of subgenus Hymenanthes. We know that Hope was an active breeder of deciduous azaleas and he made a number of selections, and a few hybrids, from species in subgenus Rhododendron, particularly in subsection Triflora.

I can also report that we are about to start an active programme of propagation, supported by several of our nurseryman friends to ensure the continuity of this most important group of hybrids and as an acknowledgement of the debt we owe to a great gardener.

Mark Flanagan is Keeper of the
Gardens, Windsor Great Park

SUMMER-FLOWERING MAGNOLIAS

MAURICE FOSTER

A thirteenth century song says that summer begins with the cuckoo's call, *"Sumer is icumen in, lhude sing cuccu…"* and we all know that the cuckoo comes in April and sings his loud song in May. This is also when *Magnolia wilsonii* flowers, generally regarded as the first of the 'summer flowering' species and the harbinger of what, rather engagingly, J.G. Millais described as the 'scarce season' for magnolias. It seems an appropriate time to begin our summer story.

The magnolia 'scarce season' of summer cannot begin to compete with the brilliant overpowering flower effects of the precocious spring magnolias. Flowers on the summer magnolias are generally more sparse and scattered, appear with the leaves, are sometimes obscured by them and rarely colour the whole bush.

However, in the garden they enjoy considerable advantages over their spring brethren. They have a prolonged period of flower often extending over a period of weeks, not to say months. They escape spring frosts and the whole display is rarely spoiled by bad weather. Many have magnificent individual flowers with exceptional fragrance. Some are among the finest evergreens available. A few have decorative fruits. As a group they offer a diverse and distinct range of foliage and form. They add character and personality to the garden as well as flowers, at a time when the dull canopies of the spring magnolias withdraw into anonymous obscurity.

To help to bring some order to this diversity it is convenient to divide summer magnolias into four groups.

Firstly, there are those that begin flowering in late April and continue into summer. Most of these have two of the most influential parent species in the genus in their ancestry, namely *M. liliiflora* and *M. acuminata*. They pass on late flowering and in some cases, a long season to their progeny, many continuing into June.

Secondly, there are the species in the Oyama section with their peak season in early summer. Conspicuous among these are *M. wilsonii*, *M. sieboldii*, *M. globosa* and their forms and hybrids, notably crosses with *M. obovata*.

Thirdly, there are the deciduous species planted chiefly for their foliage effect and striking individual flowers, such as *M. macrophylla* and *M. tripetala*.

Finally come the evergreen summer magnolias, including species of *Manglietia* and *Michelia*, now sunk into *Magnolia.* There are some 50 evergreen species, the most important of which for the garden is the noble and accommodating *M. grandiflora.*

Magnolia × *brooklynensis*
'Eva Maria'
(*M. acuminata* × *liliiflora*)

MAURICE FOSTER

The majority are warm temperate or sub-tropical species not hardy in the UK and spring rather than summer flowering.

Of the first group, we are all familiar with *M. liliiflora* which has never convincingly been found in the wild. Its excellent form 'Nigra' was introduced by Veitch in 1861. There are thirteen forms of *liliiflora* listed in the US, valued for their late flowering and long season, but differences between some of these are not distinct. A form called 'Reflorescens' flowers in late spring and then on and off through to August/September. 'O'Neill' has larger flowers. 'Darkest Purple' is darker and similar to 'Holland Red', which has slightly smaller flowers borne a little later. 'Nigra' itself is indispensable.

M. liliiflora is probably the most important parent of worthwhile hybrids in the genus. Crosses with *M. stellata* 'Rosea', the so-called 'Little Girls', reflect the *M. liliiflora* parent. There is a family similarity and they are frequently mislabelled in the trade. A recent survey of the original Washington plants, which are of course correctly labelled, listed 'Ann' as the earliest but the best summer 'rebloomer', 'Betty' with the biggest flowers, but inclined to flop, 'Jane' much later to flower and the most fragrant, 'Judy' the smallest bush and flower and the slowest grower and poor old 'Pinkie', the latest of all, described as a washed out light pink, 'sloppy, over blown and frowsy.' I rather take issue with this view having seen 'Pinkie' looking perky in the benign climate of the Auckland Botanic Garden, appealingly perky and definitely pink.

These hybrids were bred to be late flowering and compact; but the original plants now average 15 × 15ft after some 50 years. Their garden effect is considerable at a welcome time as they mature.

An underrated magnolia of similar pale colour to 'Pinkie' but with smaller flowers, on a shrub achieving only 8 × 5ft in Kent after 15 years, is 'George Henry Kern', also believed to be a *M. liliiflora* × *stellata* cross. It is possibly the longest flowering of all magnolias, from April into July, long after the leaves have matured. The flower is a soft mauve pink, and it is a useful and worthwhile plant, particularly for a small garden.

The second influential parent for late flowering is the yellow *M. acuminata,* along with its subspecies *subcordata*. The species ranges in North America from Ontario south to the Gulf coast, where the subspecies predominates. All yellow hybrids derive their colour from this source. Produced in May and June its flowers are small and 'gappy', with the tepals twisted and folded and appearing atop the leaves, often invisible from below. However, it passes on useful characteristics like hardiness and late flowering, qualities inherited by its crosses with *M. liliiflora* made at the Brooklyn Botanic Garden and known as the × *brooklynensis* grex. The type of this cross is the attractive and distinct 'Eva Maria' (see picture, page 15), intermediate in colour with tones of magenta and old rose suffused with yellow and green, with broader spathulate tepals and shapely flowers produced into July. It is worth a place in every collection.

At the dark end of the colour spectrum of this cross is 'Black Beauty' (× *brooklynensis* 204) with black/purple buds opening to small, narrow-tepalled gappy flowers, creamy yellow inside, which makes a nice contrast when viewed from a high vantage point. It is a collector's item. At the yellow end, an unnamed pale buff/yellow only faintly brushed with rose (× *brooklynensis* 374) has the largest flowers of the cross in a pleasing colour, broad-tepalled and showy.

'Hattie Carthan' is a second generation × *brooklynensis* hybrid, a cross between 'Eva Maria' and a sibling. It is a deep yellow touched with green and veined with old rose. It flowers late May/June with the deep green leaves, later than typical *brooklynensis* and one of the latest yellows to flower, along with 'Yellow Bird', which is 'Eva Maria' back crossed with *M. acuminata*. This has deep daffodil flowers emerging with the leaves.

These early summer yellows that flower with the foliage should be sited either as specimens to encourage low branching or where they can be viewed from above or at a distance. Close-planted or branching high in light woodland, the flowers cannot be seen from below and the trees have no merit as mere foliage plants.

Magnolias of the Oyama section with their fragrant nodding or pendent flowers and distinctive rose or red carpels begin their display in mid-May and continue into June and some into July. *M. wilsonii* is the best known, making a large spreading shrub that needs space to develop and thrives best in part shade. At the centre of the fragrant 4in pendent flowers, the stamens are usually rose red, but the depth of colour and vividness can vary from seed. The overall effect at peak flowering can be marred by the persistent browned tepals of spent flowers. It is an easy magnolia from seed and will flower in three to five years. In cold districts it can be grown on a wall, being tractable and easily tied in. I have seen such a plant presenting its flowers to perfection in a cold north Nottingham garden. *M. sieboldii* can be similarly treated.

With slightly smaller cupped and nodding flowers, *M. sieboldii* flowers at the same time, but goes on producing flowers into July. The best forms, often encountered in old gardens, have brilliant rich red carpels and are more effective than some more recent named forms that have weak rose or milky pink stamens. Multi-tepalled forms have also been selected. It is essentially a woodland plant and though hardy, its emerging buds can be vulnerable to late frosts. It is a spreading large shrub as broad as it is tall, branching freely from the base. *M. sieboldii* subsp. *sinensis* is sometimes treated as a species, sometimes as a

Magnolia 'Aaschild
Kalleberg'
(*M. obovata* ×
sieboldii) with
M. sieboldii

a large spreading
gangling shrub at its
best in light wood-
land. It flowers mid-
May into June.

Better known is
the superbly fragrant
M. × wieseneri,
introduced from
Japan in 1889. Its
large upward facing
flowers appear rather
sparsely in succession from mid-May to late
June on an ungainly stiff shrub, not easy to
grow well or propagate. New clones of this
cross have been developed and are promising
to be an improvement on the original.
Notable is 'Aaschild Kalleberg' (see picture,
above), a better grower with larger, freer
flowers, dark red stamens and excellent
fragrance. It promises to make a substantial
tree, favouring its parent *M. obovata* with
large leaves. It is hardy in Sweden, where it
was raised. Sir Peter Smithers has introduced
'William Watson', an open pollinated seedling
of *M. × wieseneri,* thought to be a backcross
with *M. obovata* and a large, fast-growing tree
with fragrant flowers similar to the parent.
Others, not yet named, are under trial.

The third species in the Oyama section is
M. globosa, which is in cultivation in two
forms, the Indian and the Chinese. The latter
is covered with a dense russet pubescence on
the shoots and young leaves and comes into
growth dangerously early. It is thus a martyr
to frost and suitable only for the mildest areas.

mere form. Dick Figlar of the Magnolia
Society has pointed to one consistent
difference – the length of the flower stalk
(pedicel), almost non-existent in the species,
can be up to almost 2cm long in subsp.
sinensis. This plant is particularly fine in the
form known as 'Grandiflora', with a larger
pendent flower up to 5in and contrasting rich
crimson carpels. 'Colossus' is a polyploid form
created by the late Augie Kehr in the United
States. The fragrant flowers are reported to be
of heavy texture and large, 5–6in in diameter,
with between 10–17 tepals and profusely
borne. It evidently merits its name.

M. sieboldii has been parent to a number
of hybrids, both chance and deliberate.
'Charles Coates', a chance cross with *M.
tripetala* at Kew, has large (up to 7in) creamy,
crumpled, fragrant, erect flowers with a nice
ring of red stamens and foliage that has
strong tripetala influence. It has two serious
weaknesses – the leaves can burn in full sun
in the south and the flowers are rather
shortlived and stay brown on the bush. It is

Magnolia 'Summer Solstice' (*M. globosa* × *obovata* pink form)

MAURICE FOSTER

The Indian form is not so foolhardy and has glabrous young shoots and a reddish pubescence on the underside of the leaf. The flowers are creamy white, about 3in across and retain a globose shape, never opening to a cup shape or flat. These are held more or less horizontally, revealing a ring of red stamens within. I have a seedling, raised from garden seed, which is brushed with pink outside and around the rim and an attractive plant, especially as it flowers in June and July.

Flowering at the same time and closely related to the Oyamas, but in a different botanical section is *M. obovata*, which makes a large tree in its native Japan. Introduced to the US in 1865, its whorls of large leaves set off the 6–8in wide richly fragrant flowers, creamy white with crimson stamens and the outer tepals often shaded pink. It is a fast-growing tree when young, eventually forming a broad crown, and there is an adolescence of some 12–15 years from seed before it begins to flower.

In addition to *M.* × *wieseneri*, *M. obovata* has produced another richly perfumed offspring, this time a cross with *M. globosa*. *M.* 'Summer Solstice' (see picture, above), selected from a row of seedlings at Windsor, is intermediate between the two parents in

growth and flower, forming a multi-stemmed upright tree attaining 25ft after 15 years. The flowers retain a broadly globose shape, with red stamens revealed within a dome of six large creamy white tepals and the three shorter outer pink tepals reflexing to the horizontal. The scent is overpowering, such that a single bloom placed in a guest's room was banished to the landing during the night.

M. tripetala would also perhaps be removed as it has a disagreeable scent. It was introduced from the eastern United States over 250 years ago and is hardy anywhere. Its very large leaves mean that it is occasionally mistaken for *M. macrophylla*, but its leaves taper to the base, while those of the latter are auricular or eared. It is a plant that needs space, making a medium-sized, often multi-stemmed, spreading tree, the leaves in whorls at the end of the branches, clustered below the large 6–8in creamy white flowers, which appear in late May or June. Its red 4in fruiting cones are often conspicuous and the form 'Woodlawn' was selected for its larger fruits. 'Bloomfield' was named with both flowers and foliage larger than the type.

Another vigorous large-leaved species, *M. officinalis,* is as its name suggests, widely cultivated in western China for its medicinal properties from its bark and flower buds and probably exploited to extinction in the wild. Discovered by Henry in 1885 it is of little horticultural merit, bearing 3–5in flowers after mid-May, which vary from creamy white or creamy yellow to reddish. They are not generously borne, nor very conspicuous. More often seen is its variety, var. *biloba,* with leaves deeply lobed at the tip. This was raised by Sir Harold Hillier from Lushan Botanic Garden seed in 1936. Although it is commonly mixed with the type in cultivated populations in Sichuan it is reported to come true from seed and I understand that recent laboratory analysis shows it to be quite distinct from the type.

Another summer species cultivated in China for medicine is *M. rostrata.* It originates in Yunnan and Myanmar, notably along the upper Salween and at relatively low altitude, so is not reliably hardy except in the milder parts of the United Kingdom. Having said that, it grew at Borde Hill and at the Hillier arboretum and was exhibited by Hilliers at Vincent Square in 1974. There is a fine specimen which flowers in June and July and fruits well at Glenarn, not far from Glasgow. Kingdon Ward described the 4–5in creamy white flowers as 'undistinguished', but the foliage is impressive. I estimated a leaf, on a vigorous seedling in moist forest in north-western Yunnan, at 28in long by 14in wide, still carrying something of the bronzed tint typical of the young foliage.

King of the large-leaved magnolias is *M. macrophylla.* An 80ft specimen at the Grand Hotel in Stresa, Lake Maggiore, one of only two trees in Italy at the time, with leaves of 24in and flowers of 12in, was cut down in 1925 to extend the building. J.G. Millais commented that, 'any true gardener would have destroyed the hotel'. I suspect he was perfectly serious. Frank Gladney, a celebrated United States magnolia enthusiast, walking near Gloster, Mississippi in February, waxed lyrical about the species, even in the dormant season:

'The sculptured beauty of these magnolias, resembling giant candelabra, creates masterpieces of abstract art. Thousands of inch-long silvery tips, soft as kittens ears, will develop into enormous leaf swirls centered with large white blossoms in May.'

Large indeed, as the fragrant flowers, sometimes with red spots at the centre, can reflex from cup shape to 12–18in across. They appear in the United Kingdom in June/July. The tree is hardy, though its long growing season can make it vulnerable to frost. The size and papery character of its leaves demand a wind sheltered site and plenty of sun, with a soil that does not dry out. A Mexican subspecies, *M. macrophylla* subsp. *dealbata* is similar and appears hardy in Cornwall; in Kent it has survived four winters to date in a sheltered corner.

A second subspecies, subsp. *ashei* occurs in the Florida panhandle and is quite distinct from the type, growing only to 15-20ft as a large shrub. The leaves are bright green, with a whitish underside and appear in whorls, giving it a distinctly tropical look. The flowers are white, smaller than the type from 6–10cm across and fragrant. It blooms when young, with flowers on 3 year old plants. It is quite hardy and a specimen in the Hillier Arboretum has grown and flowered as a quite small shrub for many years. It enjoys

Magnolia 'Nimbus' (M. virginiana × obovata)

the swamp bay magnolia locally – and hot sunshine to ripen the wood. At all events, it is widely grown in the United States, with over forty variants in the *Magnolia Checklist.* The southern form is known as var. *australis* and is more evergreen and less bushy. 'Henry Hicks' is a popular form of this, which succumbed here in Kent to a late frost. It is to be regretted that this species does not generally do well here as the combination of its dark green leaves, white beneath and small 3in cupped flowers is appealing, especially in July and August; and the fragrance is wonderfully sweet with citrus notes and arguably the most pleasing in the genus.

Something of this fragrance is picked up in a hybrid with *M. tripetala,* the veteran *M. × thompsoniana,* now almost 200 years old. This also captures the rich glossy green foliage with a glaucous reverse and flowers in succession over a long period, from June well into August. The flowers are creamy yellow with 12 tepals, the outer three held horizontally at the base of the upright inner tepals which eventually open flat. It is a spreading, gangling shrub that needs room to develop as it gains in effect with size and age. It arose here in London in 1808, noticed in a pot of *M. virginiana* seedlings by Archibald Thompson in his nursery in the Mile End Road. It is another attractive plant – for flower, fragrance, foliage and long season – that is relatively unknown and deserves to be much more widely planted. Recently registered is a new hybrid of the same parentage called 'Olmenhof', found in Belgium and said to have earlier and bigger flowers and a better habit. The newest hybrid is 'Nimbus' (see picture, above), a cross with *M. obovata,* raised in 1956 and introduced by the US National Arboretum in 1980. It

conditions similar to the type, can easily be accommodated in small gardens and merits wider planting. It flowers in May and June.

Another American native that occurs in Florida and extends north as far as Massachusetts is *M. virginiana.* It was the first ever magnolia to be introduced into the United Kingdom, in 1687, by John Bannister. There is an irony in this as *M. virginiana* is rarely seen growing well in United Kingdom conditions. It is often encountered as a straggly, scruffy semi-evergreen in need of a wash and brush-up, though Sir George Holford referred to a tree at Fairlawne in Kent in the 1920s some 40ft high with a trunk 6ft in circumference. This is a further irony as my garden borders Fairlawne and I am at present trying to establish a seedling at the third attempt. I suspect that what is required is a combination of abundant soil moisture – it is known as

MAURICE FOSTER

seems an unconscionably long time for a good plant from a deliberate cross to percolate into gardens and it is still rare. It has inherited something of the foliage – dark green, white reverse – and fragrance of *M. virginiana* and is semi-evergreen, but it is a free-growing, vigorous upright plant evidently with none of the bohemian appearance of its female parent. It flowers in late May through June and in Kent has grown to 15ft in six years.

The Freeman hybrids between *M. virginiana* and *M. grandiflora* look suspiciously like forms of *M. grandiflora,* but the female parent is *M. virginiana,* so suspicions are unfounded. From a cross made in the National Arboretum, Washington in 1930, two cultivars have been named: 'Freeman', recognised for its columnar habit, and 'Maryland', named to designate scions sent to Sir Eric Savill at Windsor in 1959. 'Maryland' is a first-class hardy magnolia in United Kingdom conditions, making a large shrub which can be persuaded onto a single stem to make a small tree. The flowers are cupped, sweetly fragrant and are produced in a first flush during July with greater freedom than typical *M. grandiflora* forms and continue into autumn. For smaller gardens, the relatively compact habit, manageable form and generosity of flower make 'Maryland' an excellent tree in the *M. grandiflora* style. After 18 years in Kent it has made a freestanding tree of some 7m, with a spread of perhaps 6m, about the size of a good flowering cherry.

There are some 175 forms of *M. grandiflora* listed in the *Magnolia Checklist,* with a wide range of form, foliage and flower. The species is said to have been introduced to France as early as 1711. While always seen at its best as a large and spectacular tree in the warmer regions of Europe like the south of France or the Italian Lakes, the great emblematic bull bay of the Southern States grows perfectly well in cool temperate conditions, though usually only attaining a smaller size at around 10m. It is eminently drought resistant.

New forms are constantly being introduced, widening the choice of foliage and habit. Nineteen are currently listed in the *RHS Plant Finder* of which six are new. 'Exmouth' and 'Goliath' are the two cultivars commonly seen on the walls of historic houses in England, but are no longer the best choice for the average garden. More accommodating are columnar, pyramidal selections, such as 'Emory', fastigiate with rich brown indumentum, 'Bracken's Brown Beauty' with excellent foliage colour and greater freedom of flower, 'Gallissonniere', that has stood the test of time in Europe since the 18th century, and 'Little Gem', smaller in all its parts, achieving 4 × 2m at nine years from a cutting. All have attractive brown indumentum, and show it off to good effect by holding the younger leaves at an upright angle to catch the light. All have the magnificent large, fragrant, cupped flowers, flattening to a saucer shape.

For sheer flower appeal, the massive blooms of 'Samuel Sommer' are without peer, achieving up to 14in across even in a cool climate. It is a tough and undemanding plant. Two varieties new to cultivation in the United Kingdom and said to have exceptional and dramatic dark coppery brown indumentum are 'DD Blanchard' and 'Kay Paris'. Whatever forms are selected for particular situations and tastes, this generous aristocrat of an evergreen tree should be more widely grown. Its virtues are many, its faults few.

In the same league for foliage, but not for flower, is the other great hardy evergreen, *M. delavayi*. Introduced from south-western Yunnan by Wilson for Veitch in 1899, it is a plant for gardens with plenty of space and for gardeners who favour form and foliage as highly as flower. The huge, leathery, matt dark sea green leaves, greyish beneath, create a tropical effect and as with *M. grandiflora*, early introductions were planted in the shelter of a wall. Some have long since outgrown their situation to billow above the shelter and seem perfectly at home in full exposure. It usually makes a huge rounded shrub as much as 10m across but can be pruned into a tree. It requires adequate shelter from strong winds. The intermittent flowers are disappointing, opening at night and lasting only a night or two before fading. They are normally ivory white, but recently red, pink and yellowish forms have been found in western Yunnan and can be seen in the Kunming Botanic Garden in Yunnan.

Of the evergreen *Michelia* and *Manglietia* types, recently sunk into *Magnolia*, most are spring flowering and fall outside the scope of this article. Many are under hardiness and garden value trial both here and elsewhere and it is hoped that many will prove cold hardy.

However, already of proven value here in Kent is *Magnolia insignis* (*Manglietia insignis*), which is proving perfectly hardy and fast growing as an upright evergreen tree achieving some 7m plus in ten years from seed, and flowering in year eight. The lanceolate evergreen foliage is dark rich green, and to date here undamaged. The flowers are about 3in across, buff-white, sometimes with reddish tints and rather sparsely borne in May and June. The banana-scented *M. figo* also survived a testing period of cold this year. It flowers in June and on into July and August with purple tinted, yellowish small flowers on a low bush. A variety, 'Purple Queen' has very dark flowers. It should be sited where it can be readily sniffed, perhaps in the shelter of a larger, even more aggressively fragrant summer magnolia to shade the scene. To complete the picture, all that is needed is a decent book and a nicely chilled sauvignon.

Maurice Foster is a former Chairman of the Group and remains a member of the Executive Committee. He is well-known as an expert on magnolias

THE BIRTH OF THE GROUP

DAVID FARNES

My passion for the genus *Rhododendron* was kindled almost instantly in April 1962 on my first visit to a Rhododendron Show in London to which my mother had sent me to find her 'some nice ones'. It was love at first sight for me and it completely changed my attitude and outlook towards gardening from then on. I was given a Yearbook as a Christmas present in 1963, joined the RHS the next year and attended my first Group garden visit in 1965. I had enjoyed visiting gardens with my parents long before my wife Eileen and I began, in 1958, to construct a garden of our own.

Between 1966 and 1972 the only contact I had with fellow rhododendron enthusiasts was during the annual spring tour of gardens, and at the shows held in Westminster where I purchased the Yearbooks. However, in the early 1970s there were murmurings of disquiet within the RHS that the Yearbooks were being produced at a financial loss and taking too much time from the RHS staff. At the 1971 Annual General Meeting of the RHS, the President announced that the Yearbooks were to be discontinued entirely because of inflation and rising costs. It was pointed out that the main body of RHS members could not be expected to subsidise a minority interest. A number of the members of the Rhododendron and Camellia Committee were not prepared to accept the disappearance of their Yearbook and agreed to subsidise, from their own pockets, the production of the books for at least the next year or two. Furthermore, it seemed that the Rhododendron Group, which had hitherto been open to all members of the RHS without any additional subscription, was in danger of being disbanded. This was the signal for the birth of the Rhododendron, Camellia and Magnolia Group as we know it today, and how I became involved.

On the afternoon of 4th May 1976, the first day of the Rhododendron Show, members of the Group, previously administered by the RHS at Wisley, were invited to attend a meeting to discuss taking over the administration and running our own affairs. There were many offers of help and Major Walter Magor was invited by the RHS to lead what would become the new autonomous Group with permission from the RHS to charge a subscription for the first time since 1939.

My own offer of help had to be put on hold because of an illness during much of 1977, but I was delighted to be invited by Walter Magor to take on the post of Hon. Treasurer on 4th January 1978, a post I held for eight years. In the first three of these I worked closely with our Hon. Secretary, John Waugh Owens. We enjoyed a perfect understanding and although there was much sorting out required to update old membership lists with incorrect addresses and the like, we rarely spoke over the telephone but kept in touch with an exchange of numbered letters, and it would be fair to say that at any given time we each knew what the other was about. This in the days before computers and emails.

Initially funds were short, and it took time to organise receipt of subscriptions. Back in 1976, an inaugural meeting and a gathering of members had been held in the gardens at Jermyns House, where Sir Harold and Lady Hillier welcomed us. After conducted tours of the gardens, we much enjoyed tea and cakes on the lawn and a plant sale raised funds, which helped to cover basic administration costs during 1977. The first annual subscriptions were due in November of that year, so when I took over as Treasurer there were funds already in the bank. In addition, as a guarantee for the next Yearbook, I was entrusted with the sum of £200, this being donations from members of the RHS Rhododendron and Camellia Committee. Later that year I was instructed to offer refunds to those members, as we were then fully solvent with all expenses paid.

The annual subscription was £3 per household; no additional charge was made for spouses (as happens with many other societies). One set of mailings – Bulletin, Notice of Meetings and Lectures, and similar – was sent to each address on the membership list.

It was determined by our new committee that the Yearbooks would only be sent to members upon receipt of their subscriptions, which is why our Group accounting date is 1st November, so that the majority of subscriptions would have been received by the time we took delivery of books dated for the following year. There was thus great activity by and between John Owens and myself; it was vital that we had a close understanding so that the books could be cleared quickly. John had recently moved home to Herefordshire to a much smaller house and a large number of packing cases

was more than just a nuisance in the pre-Christmas period for him and his wife Joan.

Here I should point out that we had no Membership Secretary in those days – John took care of this duty as well as being Hon. Secretary. Fortunately the printers were willing to deliver the number of books that were required for the Group directly to John. The remainder were sent to the RHS who would send an account to me in due course, but on more than one occasion I had to request this! The whole experience was completely new for them; for us it was not only new but vital to ensure the continuation and future success of the Group.

At about this time, the RHS were running short of storage space in the vaults at Vincent Square and discovered many cases of unopened Yearbooks from at least the past seven years. These were offered to the Group at no cost to us and another load of packing cases descended into Joan and John's house. It was agreed that we should sell them to members at cover prices plus postage, and they were advertised in the Bulletins, which by that time had begun to appear at fairly regular intervals and sent to all members.

I was saddened when John Owens decided to retire from the committee in 1981, but he had given valuable service and much time to the Group in those formative years and it was by then flourishing and in a healthy state. I decided that it would best serve the Group if I took on the role of Membership Secretary, as to a large extent responsibilities of Treasurer and Membership Secretary were closely linked. In one way it did mean more work, but in another way it saved much by avoidance of duplication and having to communicate with John over matching of subscriptions and despatch of Yearbooks.

Furthermore, the printers of the Yearbooks had been changed and they would now only be sent directly to RHS at Wisley, who in turn, had to deliver our requirement to Vincent Square. I then used to collect the books, as in those days I lived only 18 miles from London.

After I retired from the committee as an officer at the end of 1985, I continued to serve as an elected member with responsibility as 'Keeper of Yearbook back numbers', which I continued to advertise from time to time in our Bulletins. There was a fairly constant sale of around 100 copies per year, thus spreading the good name of our Group and furthering the close links between it and the publication of the Yearbooks – our *raison d'être*.

Acknowledgements.
POSTAN, CYNTHIA (1996). *The Rhododendron Story,* Chapter 15. Royal Horticultural Society RHODODENDRON AND CAMELLIA GROUP (1976-78). *Bulletins* 1–5.
Copies of these publications are available and can be obtained from the Group's Archivist, Pam Hayward.

David Farnes has been one of the longest-serving members of the Executive Committee, from which he retired in 2005. He was most recently Deputy Chairman. he is also the founder and former Chairman of the Group's Peak District Branch

Return to Arunachal Pradesh

Peter Cox

In 1965, when my wife Patricia, Peter Hutchison and I were not allowed to explore the ridge between the Kameng and Subansiri divisions of Arunachal Pradesh. Our host in Assam, Mr E.P. Gee, the well-known authority on Indian wildlife, suggested that we try for the Se La (pass) and Tawang, near the Bhutan frontier where even in those days there was a road. Yet again we were refused, no doubt due to the Indians still being in shock after the Chinese invasion of this area in 1962. The famous plant hunters Frank Kingdon Ward and Frank Ludlow and George Sherriff had explored this area thoroughly in the 1930s but as far as we knew, no rhododendron or other plant enthusiasts had been back to this area since.

My son Kenneth and Steve Hootman of the Rhododendron Species Foundation had been to Arunachal in autumn 2003 and had attempted to explore in the Mishmi area which is in the northeast corner of the state, but due to a lack of co-operation from the Mishmi people and terrible weather, they had to give up and did a quick visit to just where we were planning to go the following spring. While this 'poaching' of 'our' territory upset us a little, Kenneth was able to get a better idea of what we might be able to accomplish and plan our route with Oken, our host, so

we probably had a more successful trip than we might otherwise have had.

Patricia and I got together an excellent team totalling eight, seven from Scotland and one from Germany. Anne Chambers, John Roy and Franz Besch were all old Tibetan and Arunachal hands, Matt Heasman had made trips to Bhutan, so only Mike and Sue Thornley were newcomers to trekking in south-east Asia. Peter Hutchison, alas, thought he had better not attempt another Arunachal trip after the struggles he had with the terrain in 2002. Our staff were the excellent Katu whom we had in 2002, Rajin from New Delhi and our guide Tashi who knew the country intimately, plus some first rate boys.

Unlike with Kenneth in 2001 and Kenneth, Anne, John, Franz and myself in 2002, we were most unlikely to find anything new, but Kingdon Ward and Ludlow and Sherriff had left such exciting tales of what they had found and where they went, that we planned our treks to follow in their tracks, and very helpful they proved to be.

It was decided to attempt two treks, one to the east of the road to the Se La and the other to the west, the first mainly to see rhododendrons, the second primulas and meconopsis. The fact that the former area would be of a lower elevation and that primulas and meconopsis generally flower later than rhododendrons, made the decision to do the eastern trek first. Timing visits to the wilds of south-east Asia is always tricky on account of trying to be there after most of the snow has melted and before the monsoon has really got underway. We planned to leave home on 20th May and return on 12th June. As things turned out we were a bit late for the rhododendrons on the first trek but hit the high altitude ones on the second trek perfectly, with the primulas and the meconopsis just coming out. We did of course see many other plants in flower and Anne was thrilled to find around twelve species of *Arisaema*, which were almost absent in 2002.

After a night in a hotel overlooking the enormous Brahamaputra river in the much larger than I remember, unattractive town of Gauhati (now over a million people), we took off for a three hour drive eastwards up the Assam plain to the bridge and hence to the town of Tezpur from where we soon crossed the 'Inner Line', the crossing into Arunachal Pradesh for which permits are necessary. It is always exciting when first reaching the foothills. We stopped at the

divisional chief town of the Kameng Division of Arunachal, Bomdilla, built on a steep hillside at around 8,000ft, and then of course another stop when we spotted our first rhododendrons. I had hoped that we would see the amazing flowers of *Rhododendron dalhousiae* var. *rhabdotum* and here it was in all its glory (see picture, below), despite the rude comments Kingdon Ward made about it:

> *'I do not admire it. Remarkable as the great trumpet flowers, white banded with red are, there is something a little absurd in that military red stripe down each of its five trouser legs'.*

We were all thrilled by it anyway. It usually flowers in July at home but here it was just out in late May, quite a deep greeny yellow which will fade later. Find one species and there are many others, in this case another seven: *Rhododendron maddenii, R. edgeworthii, R. vaccinioides, R. kendrickii, R. arboreum, R. griffithianum, R. grande.* None of these were in flower here, and all were on a steep north-east-facing bank.

The amazing flower of *Rhododendron dalhousiae* var. *rhabdotum*

PETER COX

Rather to our surprise, an almost circular trek was planned for us, starting near Dirang, north-east up to the Poshing La and then back to the road near the Se La. It sounded from Kingdon Ward's description somewhat ambitious with what appeared to be some substantial climbing towards the end. The Poshing La itself is only 11,900ft and the Se La is 13,600ft. We were driven out of Dirang and some way up a very rough military track which gave us an altitudinal bonus, starting our trek at about 8,000ft. Our gang of porters did us proud in pushing the vehicles each time we got stuck and got covered with mud in the process, as some of us did too. The first rhododendrons here were white-flowered *R. lepidotum*, *R. neriiflorum* subsp. *phaedropum* (red) and *R. keysii* with its typical bicolour red and orange tubular flowers. After a night squeezed together in a hut, four of us on two wooden beds sleeping head to toe, we launched ourselves into a thoroughly wet day with the camera lens fugging up and rotten visibility. Leeches of various sizes abounded and midges towards the evening were as bad as in western Scotland. We were now into the heart of rhododendron country and it was intriguing to compare what we found with what Kingdon Ward listed in his book *Assam Adventure*.

Kingdon Ward visited the Poshing La twice, in 1935 and 1938, the first time in October, the second in May to see the flowers, returning in July to see the alpines. He trekked over the Poshing La from the north on his return from Tibet and here is his description of the long ridge that we trekked along in the opposite direction:

'*So we went down the ridge – and up, mile after mile; for the southern spurs of the mid-Himalayan ranges have been cross cut by the monsoon rains. In some places the water runs along the narrow crest of the ridge before tumbling over the side. The result has been to cut deep grooves along the ridge, with banks 12 to 15 feet high, overhung with trees. One may walk for half a mile through a tunnel whose roof is of pleached rhododendrons; their fallen flowers in spring crimson the ground like glowing embers. In some places our laden yak could scarcely squeeze between the banks. The forest in fact is built on sand. Just over the edge of the ridge grew giant rhododendrons trees forty to fifty feet high, with leaves 18 inches long. When in full bloom about April or May, the avenue is magnificent, bunches of blood red, white, sulphur yellow and purple flowers rocking and swaying amongst the foliage, and illuminating the forest as with thousands of Japanese lanterns.*'

Kingdon Ward goes on to list the species he found and this list was one of the chief reasons that I so wanted to explore this area as some of them have only been recorded much further east, even into China:

'*The species met with here are:* R. arizelum, R. falconeri, R. grande, R. sidereum, *all with big leaves and yellow flowers, and* R. hookeri, R. barbatum, R. argipeplum *and* R. arboreum, *all with smaller leaves and blood-red flowers. They all grow together in the silver fir forest, or at lower altitudes in the hemlock forest, but are eager for light. So overwhelming are they, that when in flower they blind one to everything else.*'

Around the Poshing La and above the pass he recorded *Rhododendron praestans*, a Chinese species.

It so happens that since Kingdon Ward's day, new species have been described that had been considered as endemic to Bhutan in the *Flora of Bhutan* Volume 2, Part 1. These are *R. flinckii*, *R. bhutanense* and *R. kesangiae*. It is the last that concerns us on

PETER COX

The white form of *Rhododendron kesangiae*

this trek. Later we saw the other two in quantity on our second trek further west. Kenneth and Steve found these three species to be common even near the road to the Se La and Tawang, and we found them in quantity elsewhere. As expected, the first big-leaved species we came across was the typically low-elevation *R. grande* with quite a wide leaf, shiny above and plastered silver indumentum below. Then *R. falconeri* subsp. *eximium* less tree-like than subsp. *falconeri* and with leaves with some persistent rusty indumentum on the upper surface and deeper cinnamon-coloured indumentum on the underside. This has a more easterly distribution than subsp. *falconeri*. Alas these two species had finished flowering. Next, to my great surprise, was typical *R. sidereum* with narrower, smaller leaves than *R. grande,* not shiny above, and

pale but clear yellow flowers. So Kingdon Ward was right on this score.

The next known *Rhododendron sidereum* occurs at the other (east) end of Arunachal in the Delei Valley. To our delight there was also *R. kesangiae* in quantity with large trusses of flowers opening pink, fading to white (see picture, above), so this would fit neatly into var. *album,* which is recorded in nearby east Bhutan. So how do our four big-leaved species compare with Kingdon Ward's? My guess is that he did not see what he called *R. arizelum* and *R. falconeri* in flower and assumed they would be yellow-flowered from what he had seen or heard of elsewhere, though *R. arizelum* is much more commonly pink than yellow, a colour which I have yet to see in the wild. So does Kingdon Ward's *R. arizelum* equal our *R. kesangiae* ? Very questionable as they are so

The epiphytic *Rhododendron megeratum*

PETER COX

yaks and cattle) carrying our kit were away on ahead, so our guide Tashi and the boys were sent ahead to bring the dzos back. In the meantime we had plenty to do.

Rhododendron hookeri amazed us, not for its flowers, as we only found two remaining trusses – both good reds, but for the size and quantity of the plants. There was a bit of a debate as to what the height of the biggest was. Mike said 50ft, I thought 45ft at most. The trunks were up to two feet wide and it might have been the commonest species in this forest. At home we regard it as a rather rare species and a bit tender, but in its best forms, unsurpassed for the glory of its scarlet flowers. We did not see anything close to *R. barbatum;* all had some indumentum, were ultra bristly and were really nearer *R. erosum* with its cordulate-based leaves than the more *R. barbatum*-like *R. argipeplum.*

There were plenty of other species to attend to. The epiphytic *Rhododendron megeratum* (see picture, left) was very common in large bunches hanging from the trees. Here was further proof that all western plants of this species have cream rather than yellow flowers, with a small yellow blotch or spotted orange. Other epiphytic species were one- occasionally to three-flowered *R. edgeworthii,* nice *R. lindleyi, R. leptocarpum* not quite out, and a few *R. camelliiflorum,* the furthest east that this species has been recorded. At 9,700ft grew clumps of very large-leaved and handsome *R. maddenii* still in tight bud. In a more open scrubby area grew *R. triflorum,* one plant being particularly good with large clear yellow flowers, interestingly with a non-peeling bark as in Tibet.

Our last day on this trek was a question of descent; in all some 4,800ft. There was plenty of interest on the way, down a

dissimilar. Some plants have the strange rim of indumentum around the leaf margin as with semi-mature *R. protistum.* To confuse matters further, there were numerous natural hybrids between *R. kesangiae, R. sidereum* and *R. falconeri* subsp. *eximium.*

The following day, Patricia became slower and slower, but eventually we made our lunch stop. We were now at 11,000ft and it became apparent that she was not going to be able to go on, as she was having difficulties in breathing at this altitude. After a long discussion, we decided to return although we did take a different route down to the valley. There is always a great discrepancy between the number of hours the locals take to walk a certain distance and what we do. At best, without stopping to botanise, we would take twice as long, but with our frequent stops it is more like three times as long. Our dzos (crosses between different path to the one we came up on. There were many bushes of *Magnolia globosa* but none had flowers fully out. Before we started to descend we had to climb up a ridge and then skirt around the edge of a very steep hillside. Above the path were masses of the white-flowered *Rhododendron lepidotum* in full sun and exposure where it would get quite dry in winter. This was voted plant of the day above a perfect *R. dalhousiae* var. *rhabdotum* epiphytic on an oak tree. It was at eye-level so perfect to photograph. On the way we passed some *R. maddenii* Polyandrum Group with flowers a good pink when first out, fading to white. These flowers were covered in small flies, which appeared to be damaging the corollas.

It soon become apparent that Mike was the fittest of us by far. He was so interested in so many things, especially as it was his first trip out east. Frequently he would be left away behind the rest of us, often catching butterflies in his net, which he would draw and then let go. Sometimes our boys would catch some for him just using their hands. And of course he also drew many of the buildings, as he is an architect by trade, as is his wife Sue, who took the photographs.

We had a rest day in Dirang and stocked ourselves up with some very welcome beer while our staff went shopping for provisions for our second trek starting the next day.

Discussions indicated that this trek would take as many as eight days at the speed that we go at, so if we had not cut the first trek short, we would not have had time to walk the second and do our trip to Tawang. Patricia had already decided that she could not manage this trek, especially as we would be going much higher, to near 15,000ft. She drove with us to the first camp and then returned to Dirang. To my surprise we set off in the opposite direction to the one I had expected, starting by going south before turning right off the main road. This was a new road in the process of construction, which will eventually join up with the other road in the north. Our first stop was at another amazing collection of rhododendrons, where we saw no less than 13 species. At the second stop, we saw five more, and at the third stop two more. New species for this trip were *R. thomsonii*, *R. cinnabarinum* (orange flowered) and *R. glaucophyllum* var. *tubiforme*.

Our camp was on a wet meadow surrounded by forest containing yet more species: *R. campylocarpum*, *R. hodgsonii*, *R. bhutanense*, *R. wallichii*, *R. flinckii*, *R. fulgens*, *R. wightii*, *R. anthopogon* and *R. fragariflorum* – just about all the remaining species we were hoping to find. This made a total for the day of 29 rhododendron species, not a bad haul! This meadow is now known as Naga GG, a name contrived by the Indian Army. To our delight, much of the meadow was covered with primulas, a dwarf yellow one which we later saw on every wet meadow, *Primula dickieana,* but also masses of the really special *P. kingii* with pendulous, deep velvety blackish claret flowers, a wonderful colour. *P. kingii* was grown very successfully by the Sherriffs in their garden at Ascreavie, Angus, but they subsequently lost it when it failed to set seed. Kingdon Ward reported finding a meadow full of it about here, so it might well have been the same meadow as we failed to find the species again.

Poor Anne discovered to her horror that her kit bag had been left behind in Dirang so she had to return with a rather tearful Patricia for the night and come back early in the morning before we set off on our trek. She made it in good time. This time we had ponies instead of dzos. Although the day started bright it soon misted over, so yet again we felt claustrophobic and down came the rain again. Somehow our staff managed to get three fires going for a late lunch, which warmed and cheered us all up. We camped near to some *Rhododendron bhutanense* (see picture, opposite), which surprised us in their colour, being mostly very deep, an almost bluish red (see picture, opposite). *R. flinckii,* to our joy, was all pale yellow-flowered and none of the off-whites or pale pinks we have seen in cultivation. *R. wightii* was as we expected and not the awful cultivated plant that we all used to call this species. The flowers were mostly over, but what we saw were hardly yellow, more of a cream. We camped near a, largely waterproof, grazer's hut and had a good meal. Katu and his team had learned a lot about our food requirements since 2002.

The next day was again damp and misty – will we ever see the countryside properly? A really good find was what we are calling *Meconopis grandis* aff, which appears to be the same taxon that Sherriff collected under the number 600 and the plants in cultivation are now known as George Sherriff Group. These meconopsis were generally growing under the protection of a deciduous berberis; later we found a few in flower, typically tinged purple in the bud opening to blue. Being near the Bhutanese frontier, we were not far from where L&S 600 and Betty's so called 'Dream Poppy' were found. There was also the yellow flowered *M. paniculata* growing in huge quantities on the steeper hillsides but very few had come into flower. Primulas became more and more plentiful, masses of the

vigorous yellow *Primula calderiana* subsp. *strumosa,* an unusual improved form of the ubiquitous *P. sikkimensis,* the little *P. glabra* with tiny pinkish purple flowers and the attractive *P. gambeliana* with flowers of various versions of purple. Two species of juniper grew into trees: the well-known *Juniperus recurva* with pendulous growth and *J. pseudosabina* with more bushy shoots. We had our tents pitched just before the rain started again.

At 4.15 in the morning shouts came from Anne to say that it was clear. I jumped out of my sleeping bag at once in case the mist rolled in again. What a joy to be able to see all the surrounding peaks and the nearby lake. To the west there was a haze of pink *Rhododendron bhutanense* stretching as far as the eye could see, right to the summits of the closest peaks. To the east was a dark rocky peak with streaks of snow. It was a great surprise that there was very little snow, even on the larger peaks of some 16,000ft. We decided to spend two nights here and do a circular trek up over the pass and around the back of the nearest mountains. Although we saw some mist hovering around, from now on we had glorious clear days and almost no more rain. I went down to the lake as I had seen some wildfowl flying past and found three adults and nine ducklings of the Ruddy Shelduck. Later, there was one probable Barheaded Goose.

We climbed to almost 14,000ft, and although there were more primulas, the other alpines were disappointing, nothing like as good as those I have seen in Tibet and Yunnan. One meadow was covered with a mass of *Rhododendron anthopogon,* all a uniform deep pink like the award of merit clone from L&S 1091, which I named 'Betty

The striking flowers of the little-known member of Subsection Taliensia, *Rhododendron bhutanense*

PETER COX

Graham', Betty Sherriff's maiden name. We climbed up to one of the most beautiful lakes I have ever seen surrounded by firs and rhododendrons including some especially fine *R. flinckii.* From here we descended steeply through a forest and *R. hodgsonii* in full flower, all good deep shades. Underneath I discovered hundreds of tiny seedlings of the rhododendron, some with only their cotyledons. The next morning it was even more crystal clear than the day before and the four of us who were Tibetan veterans reckoned we could see the sharp peak of Namcha Barwa away in the east by the great bend of the Yarlung Tsangpo.

This part of Arunachal is so different from the near perpendicular country we were exploring in 2002. It is more of a plateau with small peaks, flat watery meadows and several tarns or what we would call lochans in Scotland, often surrounded by quantities of the pink to near-red *Rhododendron bhutanense* and *R. anthopogon.* The meadows were usually covered in tufts with primulas and the very dwarf *R. fragariflorum* with pinky purple, rather untidy flowers. We would never have been able to find our way without our guide Tashi who often helped

me out by carrying my small rucksack. We passed several grazer's shielings surrounded by hard grazed meadows and the occasional small herd of yaks. Sometimes the paths were either hard to follow or virtually non-existent. Often it was a question of jumping from stone to stone or tuft to tuft. We once came across a patch of cut-over *R. bhutanense,* no doubt to increase the area of grazing, but on the whole the pressure on the native flora is not too severe away from roads and villages.

One night we camped lower down by a river at 12,100ft where it was much warmer, expecting a hard climb back up to the plateau again the next day, but it turned out quite easy. There were few new plants as their habitat did not vary much. Once we came across a small population of clear yellow *Fritillaria cirrhosa,* a species that is widespread and often flecked with purple or green. On one pass was a gorgeous little primula with deep purple pendulous flowers, only two plants seen, *P. wattii.* There were also bluish purple *P. calderiana* in addition to the yellow subsp. *strumosa* and several hybrids in between these two. Kingdon Ward remarked on these as being deplorable, which was about true.

Our last camp was just in sight of the road where we were to be picked up but there was still some way to go. We passed through a *Rhododendron hodgsonii*-juniper-fir forest and then a pure juniper-*R. thomsonii* forest. The last steep-forested hillside facing north, near where we descended to a meadow and river, had patches of yellow *R. campylocarpum*. One *R. bhutanense* was almost white. The path was very stony and we were lucky no one twisted an ankle or worse. At last we reached the road but our staff had failed to get hold of Oken on the radio and were not sure if this was even the right day to be picked up. But within 20 minutes there was a loud cheer and there were our vehicles appearing over the horizon. We were all delighted to meet up again, especially Patricia and I.

The first part of the road was built on a most unstable often perpendicular hillside and we were relieved to get to the end of it at the Se La where we turned towards Tawang. There was a long, long drop down to the valley below Tawang where we made a small diversion to the spectacular Nuriang waterfall and then a climb up again to the surprisingly large town spread out along and up and down the hillside. I was surprised by the lushness of the vegetation here as we were now many ridges back from the plains and I had expected to be in a dry rain-shadow area. One new plant that was very common in and around Tawang was the yellow candelabra *Primula smithiana*, now sunk into *P. prolifera*. The other thing Tawang

was noticeable for was the number of dogs that carried on an endless chorus of barking at night. The town is dominated on the west side by the large monastery.

We had a day trip further west to the huge Zemithang stupa, the only others of comparable size being the Tashijangsi in Bhutan and the Bodinath in Katmandu. We had hoped to do a day's botanising, but owing to the proximity of the Bhutanese and especially the Tibetan frontier, the Indian army would not let us go any closer, which included up into the mountains. Two noteworthy plants seen *en route* were groups of the giant lily *Cardiocrinum giganteum* and the rare *Lilium nepalensis* var. *concolor*, both in full flower.

It was now near the end of our trip so we had to return to Dirang via the Se La. All the best plants seemed to be in no-go military areas where we were not allowed to stop, but we were able to spend some time around the pass and again down a bit on the south side. On the pass I searched in vain for the little pink-flowered *Rhododendron pumilum*, which Kenneth and Steve thought they had found, plus *R. nivale*, but to no avail. The former has been recorded on the Me La, which is just south of Tawang in Bhutan. The latter may prefer a drier habitat. There was plenty of high-altitude *R. lepidotum*, but the flowers were not nearly out, also *R. anthopogon*, *R. fragariflorum* and *R. bhutanense* of similar colours to those we had seen before.

Lower down, we did two short cuts between bends in the road at around 12,500ft where there were lots of *Rhododendron thomsonii* and more good orange *R. cinnabarinum*. I had intended that we make a stop lower down to look for the tender species again, especially

R. boothii, which we had failed to find on this trip, but it mostly looked too dry for epiphytic species. We did notice some *R. maddenii,* pale pink fading to white as before, and a lot more roscoeas, these white with a purple centre.

Overall it had been a great trip except for poor Patricia missing the second trek, which I am sure she would have enjoyed if she had been fit enough. The difference from the first jungly trek to the open plateau of the second was startling, as was the sudden clearing of the weather to give us great visibility. Most of us had known each other beforehand and we turned out to be a very congenial party. The final plant of the trip was *Rhododendron anthopogon,* which was well deserved.

Peter Cox, a Director of Glendoick Gardens Ltd, Glencarse, Perth, is extremely well known for his writing on rhododendrons and for his many plant-hunting trips to China and countries of the Himalaya region

KUNMING REVIVAL

BRIAN WRIGHT

In May 2005 the Group presented fifteen varieties of *Camellia reticulata* – so called Kunming cultivars – to Abbotsbury Gardens. This donation represents the largest collection of these plants growing anywhere in the UK and possibly the whole of Europe. If this sounds like an interesting conservation project, as well it might be, conservation is not really the subject of this offering. I hope it's more about why these camellias and particularly their hybrids are not more widely available and more widely grown in this country. After all, they are of intriguing historical interest and spectacularly bold and beautiful in flower. They are also rewarding in that they can be somewhat, but not overwhelmingly, challenging to grow – and, of course, they're something with which to impress your friends.

Since, in relation to the 'Kunmings', I have already mentioned 'their hybrids', you will know at once that my title is not at all confining. I suppose it was never meant to be as this race of camellia, in the first place, grows in gardens, especially temple gardens, in regions of Yunnan other than Kunming – and probably has done for over a thousand years. And 'Revival' is used more in hope (at least in this country) than actuality. But still, with what is to follow, you might agree that 'Kunming Revival' is as good as any place to start.

Virtually everyone who reads this Yearbook will know that the first 'Kunming', or rather Yunnan, reticulata, 'Captain Rawes' (see picture, below left), arrived on these shores in 1820. This was, and probably still is, the best known and

Camellia 'Captain Rawes', the first reticulata to be introduced to the UK in 1820

The Abbotsbury plant of the double-flowered *Camellia* 'Robert Fortune' (syn. 'Pagoda')

Camellia 'Milo Rowell' ('Crimson Robe' x
C. *japonica* 'Tiffany') – reticulata hybrid from
the Antony House collection

Camellia 'Shot Silk' (Award of Merit 1952)

most famous of all the reticulata cultivars. Indeed, many fine specimens are still to be found growing in Cornish gardens while two of the oldest known plants survive well outside at Leonardslee in Sussex and under glass at Chatsworth House, Derbyshire. A second introduction of this reticulata was made by John Damper Park for the RHS in 1824 but it wasn't until the great plant hunter, Robert Fortune, introduced the prolifically flowering dark pink formal double, 'Flore Pleno', in the late 1840s or 1850s that anything more sensational occurred. Better known as 'Robert Fortune' or 'Pagoda' (see picture, opposite) or any one of at least three other synonyms, it seems that this camellia may well have been introduced much earlier, since it was reported in Curtis's Botanical Magazine of 1857 that a mature specimen, which was relieved of some 2000 buds in October 1848, still flowered profusely, from as many buds again, the following spring.

Anyhow, apart from George Forrest sending wild-collected seed to England in 1924 while apparently ignoring the garden forms, which one feels that he must have encountered, and which are germane to this article, nothing more happened for 100 years.

Then from 1948 to 1950, the two American authorities, Dr Walter Lammerts and Mr Ralph Peer, succeeded in importing consignments of reticulatas from China. I say 'succeeded' as the search for these plants required much effort, expenditure and prolonged negotiations (see my article in the March 2003 Bulletin). Eventually, however, contact was made with Mr Te-Tsun Yu – he of that well-documented address on *Camellia reticulata* and its garden forms given at the RHS Camellia & Magnolia Conference in 1950 – and Professor H.T. Tsai. At the time, the former was the Director of the Yunnan Botanical Institute in Kunming and the latter his assistant. The happy consequence of West meeting East was that some twenty different

Camellia 'Purple Gown'   Camellia 'Noble Pearl'

'Kunming' varieties (or so it was thought at the time) were sent to California. This was the beginning of a huge universal interest in these plants since (a) they were quickly propagated and generously distributed to many parts of the camellia-growing world, and (b) later used in various hybridisation programmes.

Mr Hope Findlay, in his 1964 Yearbook article, talks of 'Kunmings' arriving in England as early as 1951 and of Wisley receiving an Award of Merit for 'Shot Silk' (see picture, previous page) in 1952. At about the same time or shortly after, Bodnant also received a supply, for in the 1956 Yearbook, Charles Puddle mentions them flowering there for the third time. He describes 'Purple Gown' (see picture, above), 'Moutancha', 'Pagoda', 'Butterfly Wings', 'Tali Queen' 'Noble Pearl' (see picture, above), 'Lionhead', 'Chang's Temple' and 'Cornelian'. He talks of them growing in the open and of being strong growers.

In 1956, Ralph Peer presented twelve 'Kunmings' to The Crown Estate, Windsor.

They were planted in the then Temperate House in Savill Gardens. Writing in his 1964 Yearbook article mentioned above, Hope Findlay regarded 'Chang's Temple', 'Cornelian' and 'Willow Wand' as being poor doers and eliminated them from the collection. The remaining nine grew on to become sturdy plants but were lost in 1987 when the great storm wrecked the Temperate House and the plants had to be cut down after attempts at transplanting them failed.

Of the plants received by Wisley possibly only 'Butterfly Wings' survives. Each Spring, in full bloom, it presents a glorious sight in the entrance to the main greenhouse.

During the 1950s 'Kunmings' must have also arrived at some of the great Cornish gardens since mature specimens can still be seen in the open at Caerhays, Trewithen, Mount Edgecumbe and Antony House. As the decade moved on to the 1960s it became clear that, due to incorrect labelling and some plants carrying as many as three different names, some adjustments had to be made in

Camellia 'Royalty' (*C. japonica* 'Clarise Carleton' x 'Chang's Temple')

Camellia 'Francie L' ('Apple Blossom' x 'Buddha')

order to establish true identities. The task of doing this was undertaken by the eminent New Zealand expert Colonel Tom Durrant. After some intensive research and global enquiry, Tom Durrant not only brought order to what was becoming a most confused state of affairs but also discovered that the number of different varieties that were earlier imported by Lammerts and Peer was considerably less then the twenty thought at the time. However, by 1964, Tom Durrant received a further shipment of reticulatas from Kunming, several of which had never before been seen outside China.

Below is a nomenclature list, which derives from Tom Durrant's work. It names 21 plants, plus 'Captain Rawes', that are believed to be in cultivation in the West today; it was this list that the Group worked from in the search for the 15 plants presented to Abbotsbury.

The interest in Yunnan reticulatas and their hybrids had reached such a height that from the sixties to the eighties good listings

were being offered by specialist nurseries across the world. The UK was no exception and among the front-runners was James Trehane & Sons who were listing up to 29 varieties, two of which were of pure Yunnan origin.

Today, in this country, the *RHS Plant Finder* lists some nine nurseries who advertise reticulatas but on enquiry one finds that each sell barely a handful. Loder Plants does best by offering eight, three of which are the real McCoy and named in the list on page 41.

If you want absolute choice, you would need to shop abroad e.g. Europe, Australia, New Zealand, USA or, of course, China. In my experience, Nuccio's of California is the best bet. Reticulata-wise they catalogue over 70 hybrids, named seedlings and pure 'Kunmings'.

So why don't we do better here? Some, with far more experience than I, will say they're not so easy to propagate. But the Chinese have been doing so for centuries and with modern techniques and some fairly talented plantspeople about we could do better. Others will say that outside the South West Peninsula they're not so hardy. Well, the late John Hilliard grew an enviable collection, with the flimsiest of protection, in his Crawley, Sussex garden. So too does Andy Simons in Bedfordshire (Bedfordshire! That's almost exposed East Anglia). In Surrey, Wisley grow a good-sized 'Royalty' (see picture, previous page) up on the hardly sheltered Battleston Hill and for 20 years or more Everard Daniel has reared a superb 'Francie L' (see picture, previous page) on his house wall in Reigate, while over in Worplesdon, Surrey, Roderick White is building a fine open-grown collection. Up on higher ground in Kent, the Fosters grow 'Royalty' (see picture, previous page) and 'Satan's Robe' while I, on a Sussex elevation grow 'Arbutus Gum' and 'Arch of Triumph'; this pair have been outside for twelve years and season after season reward me with an abundance of hefty blooms. And further north, I know that reticulatas grow in parts of the Midlands and Cheshire.

Ideally, these plants do require some shelter but in spite of this they should be better known and more widely grown.

This winter, as you browse through this Yearbook, consider the 'Kunmings', their seedlings and hybrids. The possibility is that a 'Kunming Revival' won't be such a pipe dream after all.

Footnote: In her book, *Camellias,* Jennifer Trehane states that at the Kunming Institute of Botany there are five times as many different Yunnan reticulata cultivars growing than are listed on the opposite page. If this is the case, it reveals that if we, in Britain, could run before we could walk, we would have an awful lot to go at.

Brian Wright is a member of the Group's Southeast Branch and also of the Executive Committee. He developed the project of planting a collection of 15 Kunming reticulatas at Abbotsbury Garden in May 2005

Yunnan *Camellia reticulata* cultivars believed to be in cultivation in the West (ie. including Australia & New Zealand)	
Trade or Western name	**Pin-yin or Chinese synonym**
*'Chrysanthemum Petal'	Juban
*'Robert Fortune' (syn. 'Pagoda')	Songzilin
*'Shot Silk'	Dayinhong
*'Purple Gown'	Zipao
*'Butterfly Wings'	Houye Diechi
*'Crimson Robe'	Dataohung
'Moutancha'	Mudan cha
*'Professor Tsai'	Yinhung Diechi
'Lionhead'	Shizitou
*'Cornelian'	Damanao
*'Chang's Temple'	Zhangjia cha
'Osmanthus Leaf'	Xiaoguiye
'Takueiyeh'	Daguiye
*'Willow Wand'	Luanye yinhong
*'Tali Queen'	Dali cha
*'Noble Pearl'	Baozhu cha
'Early Crimson'	Zaotaohung
'Early Peony'	Zaomoudan
*'Buddha'	-
*'Confucius'	-
*'Spinel Pink'	Mayehyinhung
plus 'Captain Rawes'	Guixia

*Presented by the Group to Abbotsbury.
'Spinel Pink', or Mayehyinhung, is probably synonymous with 'Shot Silk'.

FORGOTTEN PLANTS

Magnolia × *soulangeana* 'Triumphans'

Triumphans [*M.* × *soulangeana*], cv. (Bosse, Vollst. Handb. Blumeng., Ed. 2, 2: 467. 1841), name in catalogs as *M. triumphans;* in Loudon, Hort. Brit. 584 (1850); syn.: *M. conspicua* cv. Triumphans (Mouillefert, Traite 119. 1891), petals red on exterior at base and along midribs, cites cv. Grandis in synonymy. in Wyman, Arnoldia 20: 28 (1960), resembles cv. Rustica (Rubra).[1]

'Triumphans' White buds opening to white flowers with red stripes down the centre of the tepals and at the base, A French clone named ca. 1891.[2]

'Triumphans' is a goblet shaped rose-red flower with a pinkish-white interior. The flowers are seen in mid April. This early 19th century clone has small pinkish red flowers seen in abundance towards the end of the *M.* × *soulangeana* flowering period.[3]

These references make bald reading and would not encourage even the most avid collector to seek out this cultivar. The only specimen I know is on Battleston Hill in the RHS garden at Wisley in southern England.

When I first saw it some years ago I was, admittedly, suffering from severe delusion about the performance of my true *Magnolia* × *soulangeana* 'Lennei' at home. Its flowers had promised much that spring, but once again every one emerged showed black staining from wind and cold damage in bud, and the tree insisted on growing like a perverted corkscrew: I am sure you all find this cultivar

Magnolia × *soulangeana* 'Triumphans'

wonderful, but the only perfect flowers I have seen have been in kinder climes abroad.

However, shortly afterwards at Wisley, the sight of a magnificent mature 'soulangeana type' magnolia covered in deep pink bloom and growing with due regard to gravity was a positive tonic. What was it? One of Amos Pickard's best selections? A hybrid of 'Iolanthe'? Something new from the USA or New Zealand? No, it was a cultivar from France raised 150 years before. What a nice surprise.

In spite of Jim Gardiner's description[3], the flowers that year were a good size and a good colour, more pleasing to me than that other 'Lennei' alternative *Magnolia* 'Rustica Rubra': the growth habit is denser and the

MIKE ROBINSON

flowers are a more even colour. Every year I have seen it since has been just as good.

With excellent purple flowers on modern cultivars such as *Magnolia* 'Apollo' there is not room for *M.* 'Rustica Rubra' or *M.* 'Lennei' in my garden, but there will always be a place for *M.* 'Triumphans'. I commend it to you.

References

[1] Magnolia Society International cultivar checklist – **www.magnoliasociety.org**

[2] CALLAWAY D. (1994) *Magnolias.* Batsford. 207

[3] GARDINER J.M. (2000) *Magnolias: A Gardener's Guide.* Timber Press. 277, 280

Dr Michael Robinson became Chairman of the Group in 2004 and is a former Chairman of the Southeast Branch. He gardens in the Ashdown Forest and has a fine collection of both magnolias and rhododendrons

Hydrangeas as Companion Plants

Shelagh Newman

Hydrangea aspera 'Macrophylla'

Ten years ago, the genus *Hydrangea* would not have figured in a list of my 'top ten' plants. Rhododendrons would have been close to the top, as would camellias and magnolias, but hydrangeas? Were they not those rather ubiquitous plants which in late summer, in varying shades of lurid pink or pale blue, spilt over the red brick walls of seaside front gardens. Floriferous, yes; reliable, perhaps; certainly useful as late summer colour, but exciting must-have plants – never. That was until I became involved, as a volunteer gardener, with the National Collection of Hydrangeas held by the Lakeland Horticultural Society at its garden at Holehird, Windermere. The Society is a registered charity and its 10-acre gardens, manned entirely by enthusiastic volunteers, are open to the public from dawn to dusk, funded by donation.

The National Collection of *Hydrangea* was established at Holehird by Toni Lawson-Hall and the late Brian Rothera in 1989. I joined the team in 1996, taking over as its sole custodian three years ago when Toni Lawson-Hall moved south to be closer to her family.

My close contact with this genus – we now have 13 species and 249 cultivars and subspecies in the Collection – has made me realise that they are seriously underrated and undervalued plants. Many are little known and rarely grown. As an enthusiastic grower of rhododendrons, camellias and magnolias, I am increasingly realising their value as companion plants.

There are a number of reasons why hydrangeas provide a perfect partnership with our three genera:

Firstly, the season of flowering of hydrangeas is complementary. As the last flowers of rhododendrons fade in June the first hydrangea flowers begin to open. The flowering succession of species and cultivars continues throughout July, August and September continuing until the first frost, often in November, when the first blooms of *Camellia sasanqua* and *Rhododendron* 'Nobleanum' appear.

Secondly, they enjoy similar cultural conditions. The areas of China, Korea, the Himalaya and Japan, where many species of rhododendron, camellia and magnolia occur naturally, are also home to hydrangea species *H. heteromalla, H. aspera, H. serrata, H. paniculata* and *H. macrophylla.* They enjoy the same, moist, shaded woodland conditions and humus-rich soils. These acidic soils enable the full colour range of

Hydrangea serrata 'Blue Deckle'

SHELAGH NEWMAN

H. macrophylla cultivars to be enjoyed. In the garden they can be planted together without any cultural modifications. In the western hemisphere, the south eastern states of the USA, where the occidental azaleas and magnolias occur, is home also to *H. arborescens* and *H. quercifolia.*

Aesthetically, they blend well together, too. With the exception of one or two climbers, hydrangeas are deciduous – offering no distraction from the spring evergreen beauty of the rhododendrons and camellias. The scale of the plants is similar, too; varying from the large *H. heteromalla* and *H. aspera* species and cultivars to small *H. serrata* plants and the suckering *H. involucrata,* there is a hydrangea the right size and shape for any situation.

So why has the hydrangea not been espoused with the same enthusiasm as the other three genera? Why has it never been deemed worthy of a society devoted to its cause? I suspect that one of the main reasons is the widespread perception by the public of

SHELAGH NEWMAN

Hydrangea serrata 'Grayswood'

the 'hydrangea'. It is perceived as either a rather indifferent 'mophead' *H. macrophylla* in the garden, or as a colourful house plant. Very few of its more interesting species and cultivars appear to have, in the past, impinged on the public imagination. The horticultural trade must bear some of the blame for this state of affairs. There are now some excellent small nurseries which are stocking good, named plants, but too frequently in the past, *H macrophylla* cultivars have been labelled simply as such, sometimes with a colour specified but rarely with a cultivar name supplied. There are, also, few garden centres and nurseries which stock a wide variety of different hydrangea species and their cultivars. To find good and unusual plants the *RHS Plant Finder* must be consulted and perhaps a degree of effort undertaken to source the plant – but then that is surely part of the enjoyment of acquiring the rare and unusual. The hydrangeas that I shall recommend as companion plants are all commercially available according to the 2005–2006 edition of the *RHS Plant Finder.*

Hydrangea macrophylla

These types originate from the maritime regions of Japan and occur as 'lacecap' or 'mophead' forms. They may be the most commonly grown, but they cannot all be dismissed as unmemorable; some cultivars are better than others.

The species itself is rarely seen but makes an attractive garden plant, especially in its lacecap form. The acid soils favoured by rhododendrons lend themselves to a particularly wide colour range in *H. macrophylla* and *H. serrata* cultivars – the only species where the colour changes with soil pH. White-flowered plants and some red ones will retain their colour regardless of soil. Blue- and purple-flowered plants will only occur on acid soils in the presence of available aluminium, giving a wide choice of colours to use.

Some particularly desirable lacecap forms were bred at Wadenswil in Switzerland in the 1980s. Selected for the intensity of their sepal colour, they are referred to as the Teller Series and were named, in German, after birds. Good examples are *H. macrophylla* 'Möwe' (purple), 'Rotschwanz' (red), 'Blaumeise' (blue) and 'Bläuling' (pale blue).

Recommended 'mophead' forms include two less common plants bred in the USA, 'All Summer Beauty' (pale blue on acid soil), which flowers from June until the first frosts, and 'Oregon Pride', which has intense purple flowerheads on acid soil supported by black stems. 'Parsival', mauve with a blue eye, has a particularly attractive near-spherical flowers and, when available, 'Ave Maria' is a floriferous but small to dwarf, white-flowered plant. *H. macrophylla* cultivars require annual pruning in spring to retain a good shape and health, and they are therefore suited to the more formal areas of the garden and where time constraints are not too important. They would combine well with hybrid rhododendrons and with magnolias. White lacecap varieties such as 'White Wave' or 'Lanarth White' look particularly well when grown adjacent to the brown leaf rhododendrons such as 'Elizabeth Lockhart' or *R. bureavii,* with its rust-coloured indumentum. Similarly, the new silver foliage and fawn indumentum of *R. pachysanthum* blends well with blue flowered forms of *H. macrophylla* types.

Hydrangea serrata

The species occurs naturally in the mountainous areas of Japan where it grows in part shade. Much hybridising work has been carried out in Japan, where they are a popular plant, and some very desirable plants, many with Japanese names, are reaching this country. They are particularly suited to growing alongside Japanese azaleas and some of the smaller rhododendrons, or beneath larger magnolias. A dainty, deciduous shrub, they rarely exceed 1.5m in height, carrying many corymbs of lacecap flowers with an inner ring of fertile flowers surrounded by an outer ring of sterile flowers with showy sepals.

They tend to fall into two types: Those that are blue on acid soil and pink on alkaline, such as 'Tiara', 'Diadem', 'Miranda' and 'Blue Deckle' (see picture, page 45) tend to perform best in partial shade to prevent the sun scorching the sepals. The second type, such as 'Grayswood' (see picture, opposite page), 'Beni Gaku', 'Macrosepala', and 'Intermedia' have sepals that open white and suffuse to a deep crimson. When the fertile flowers are pollinated these sepals will reverse and take on a deeper red. These plants

Hydrangea paniculata Pink Diamond ('Interhydia')

benefit from a sunnier aspect. *H. serrata* cultivars are trouble-free, require the minimum pruning and are very suited to informal planting.

Hydrangea heteromalla

This plant, or one of its cultivar forms such as 'Yalung Ridge' or 'Snowcap', is well suited to combining with the bigger species rhododendrons in larger gardens. A large shrub, it was introduced into cultivation from China and the Himalayas in 1880, and it has hairy leaves and large cream lacecap flowers in June. It requires no pruning and little attention.

Hydrangea involucrata

At the other end of the height scale, this species from Japan is a small, suckering plant rarely seen in gardens, with small lacecap flowers comprising white outer florets around violet fertile flowers and heart-shaped green leaves. It should definitely be grown more frequently. It flowers profusely over a long period and is eminently suitable for planting in front of spring-flowering shrubs; it would also slot very comfortably into an herbaceous border. In colder districts it is happier in a sheltered position, but it has survived numerous Cumbrian winters! The species itself is very attractive and there is also a double form 'Plena' as well as a number of cultivars, the most readily available of which is 'Hortensis'.

Hydrangea arborescens

This species would grace any herbaceous border, particularly the cultivars 'Annabelle' and 'Grandiflora'. A native of the southern United States, it is a suckering plant, but it does not appear to be particularly invasive here. The huge flowerheads open lime green and age to cream; the plant also has a long flowering season, from midsummer until the first frosts. In areas of high rainfall, where the huge flowerheads can be weighed down, it is wise to keep pruning to a minimum, leaving some woody stems to support the heavy flowerheads. A smaller cultivar, *H. arborescens* subsp. *discolor* 'Sterilis' is equally attractive but does not suffer this problem, making it more suited to wet areas. These plants look spectacular when planted in front of large rhododendrons with a smaller one in front to cover the bare stems early in the year. The dark leaves act as a foil to the white flowerheads, which in turn lighten a dark area when the rhododendrons have finished flowering.

Hydrangea paniculata

So named for the long, white or cream panicles that it bears from July until October, this plant occurs widely in the Far East in China, Taiwan and Japan. The species itself can grow up to 5m and is quite garden-worthy in its best forms. Some of the best cultivars available were bred by the de Belder family in Kalmthout, Belgium and a number have been awarded an RHS Award of Garden Merit (AGM). They include 'Kyushu', 'Unique' and 'Grandiflora'. Also worthy of space in the garden are 'White Moth', 'Pink Diamond' (see picture, previous page) and 'Burgundy Lace'. Their splendid, arching habit contrasts well with the rounded shapes of camellias and rhododendrons, and the large cream panicles add light and interest to the dark green leaves in summer. They can be pruned back quite hard early in the year, making them quite unobtrusive during the spring display of the camellias; indeed the harder they are pruned the larger the panicles they will produce. In colder areas of the country they are very reliable, flowering on the current year's growth, which does not appear until the danger of frost has passed.

Hydrangea quercifolia

The American oak leaf hydrangea is another panicle-bearing plant that is used to a continental climate of cold winters and hot summers. The species has flowered and performed well in Cumbria over the last few years. Besides its spectacular cream panicles in August and September, the leaves age to a rich red-purple in autumn. In areas of high rainfall like the Lake District, the huge panicles of cultivars such as 'Harmony' and the double 'Snowflake' get weighed down with water. The species, however, which can be found for sale in good nurseries, is a fine plant in its own right and the lighter panicles will not be so affected. For colder, damper areas the species also appears to be a hardier plant than its cultivars.

Hydrangea aspera

This is perhaps my favoured species to put in an informal woodland garden with rhododendron or camellias. A large shrub or small tree, it has a wide geographical distribution from the Himalayas to China, Taiwan and Indonesia. With its large corymbs of violet fertile flowers surrounded by lilac sterile flowers, it makes a spectacular plant for the country garden and really ought to be more widely grown. The species has produced some excellent cultivars, too. Notable among them is the AGM-awarded 'Macrophylla' (see picture, page 44); it has large velvety leaves, up to 10cm long, contrasting particularly well with the glossy dark foliage of camellias and rhododendrons. The flowering corymbs can exceed 15cm in diameter. Other, particularly worthy and obtainable cultivars include 'Peter Chappell', which has cream fertile flowers surrounded by pale pink to white sterile flowers and was named by Maurice Foster after the Spinners nurseryman, and 'Kawakami'. The latter has been crossed by the Japanese with *H. involucrata* to produce a smaller shrub (to 1.5m), which at Holehird is proving very floriferous. This plant is now available through the *RHS Plant Finder* and we are propagating it at Holehird with the expectation that it will become a very desirable plant.

There are also three subspecies of the species that are worth considering: *H. aspera* subsp. *sargentiana* is a very large plant (up to 3m) with large, heart-shaped rugose leaves and white sterile flowers. It combines well with large-leaved species rhododendrons in an informal country garden setting. Less well known are *H. aspera* subsp. *strigosa* and subsp. *robusta* var. *longipes*. The latter is a smaller plant, introduced from Hupeh in north west China in 1887 and is very vigorous, producing many corymbs in June, earlier than most of the species. The many light-coloured flowers show up well against dark, evergreen foliage.

Hydrangea villosa

Previously classified as Villosa Group within *H. aspera,* it may be found in some nurseries still so labelled. Work carried out recently on the DNA by Ben Zonneveld at the Institute of Molecular Plant Sciences in Leiden, Netherlands has now shown it to be a separate species. A number of cultivars that were also considered as *H. aspera* have now been reclassified. Among these, 'Sam McDonald' and 'Mauvette' are worthy of a place in the rhododendron or camellia garden.

The *H. aspera–H. villosa* species are trouble-free, requiring pruning only when their size needs reducing, and they flower reliably even after the first leaves have been damaged by a late frost. They are fully hardy and are ideal in light woodland where they can be protected from damaging cold winds.

Cultivation of Hydrangeas

Hydrangeas suffer few cultural problems and are not time consuming plants to grow, with the exception of the *H. macrophylla* types, which require annual pruning. They are susceptible to honey fungus, like many other shrubs and trees. Some plants, but not all, are subject to attack from capsid bug. Notable among these are the species and cultivars of *H. paniculata.* Varieties of *H. paniculata* and *H. quercifolia* are subject to predation by deer and it is better not to grow these in gardens frequently visited by them.

Hydrangeas will thrive in moist humus rich soils. An annual mulch of leaf mould or home-made compost is all that is required. A mulch will also help to retain the moisture in the soil and suppress weed growth. If they are grown in a deprived soil and the leaves begin to look chlorotic, an annual top dressing of Growmore and ammonium sulphate will redress the nitrogen imbalance without raising the pH of the soil.

Conclusion

The purpose of a National Collection is to preserve as many of the species and cultivars of a particular genus as possible and to seek to distribute them to prevent their extinction to cultivation. To that end, material is made available to interested nurserymen and gardeners whenever possible. For the horticultural trade to wish to propagate and sell a variety, however, they need to be able to register a commercial demand from the gardening public. I hope I may have aroused an interest in an undervalued genus and in particular in some of its more unusual forms to include as natural and worthy companions to the rhododendrons, camellias and magnolias in our gardens.

References

HAWORTH-BOOTH, M. (1950) *The Hydrangeas.* Constable & Co.

LAWSON-HALL, T. & ROTHERA, B. (Revised 2004) *Hydrangeas: A Gardeners' Guide.* Batsford.

MCCLINTOCK, E. (1957) *A Monograph of the Genus Hydrangea.* California Academy of Sciences.

VAN GELDEREN, C. J. & D. M. (2004) *Encyclopedia of Hydrangeas.* Timber Press.

Shelagh Newman is curator of the National Collection of hydrangeas held by the Lakeland Horticulturual Society at Holehird, its garden above Lake Windermere. She has also recently become Chairman of the Lakeland Rhododendron Society and is also now a member of the Group

THE NESS HOLT HYBRID RHODODENDRONS – AN OCCIDENTAL BIRTH!

PETER CUNNINGTON

Only occasionally does a new group of deciduous *Rhododendron* hybrids enter the horticultural world and rarely do they have their origins in the north of England. There will be those, however, who might argue about the exact geographical location of Cheshire, preferring, perhaps, to place the county in the north-west Midlands. Leaving aside the regional debate, it is on Wirral in particular that we must look to find the origins of what were formerly known as the Pratt Hybrids, now more suitably designated Ness Holt Hybrids.

Montague Camden Pratt, Denny to all who knew and admired him, was a southerner by birth, the son of a Sussex medical practitioner. Choosing not to enter the medical profession, he took a degree in Botany and in 1930 was appointed to a lectureship at the Liverpool Polytechnic now John Moores University. His lively lectures were always enhanced by living material, much of which was gathered from his own garden, *Briarcroft,* of which he was inordinately proud. He was especially committed to planting flowering cherries, becoming a leading authority on their characteristic distinctions, and delighted in the underplantings of shrubs with bulbs. The garden became deservedly popular both locally and further afield, and he enjoyed nothing more than conducting groups of students and gardeners around, pointing out his specialities and enlivening his comments with appropriate anecdotes. It has been said that Denny was, *'a teacher by training and inclination but a gardener by heart'.*

It was in the late 1950s that Denny turned his interest to the breeding of

Rhododendron 'Brimstage'

Rhododendron 'Spital'

JOAN WILKINSON

deciduous azaleas. An admiration for the strong, bright colours of both Knap Hill and Exbury cultivars led him to initially cross the best of these with Ghent, Mollis and Occidentale hybrids, with a view to creating very fragrant varieties coupled with vivid colour. One such plant, later named 'Elsie Pratt' for his late wife, was enthusiastically taken up by W. de Jong and Sons of Boskoop. It is an upright plant with trusses of deep pink flowers with orange markings and a bronze flush in the young foliage. This hybrid from the Knap Hill azalea 'Les Sylphides' crossed with a pink-flowered Mollis won a silver medal at Boskoop in 1970 and a Certificate of Merit three years later after trials.

Working with staff of the neighbouring University of Liverpool's Botanic Garden at Ness, further seedlings were raised, propagated and named; significant among these, was 'Anneke' of which Denny wrote,

'I have compared its pure golden, large flowers with the Azaleas of Exbury and feel confident that

it will hold its own place alongside the other Knaphills.'

Originally named 'Gold N' he felt that it would be unwise for it to be confused with a brand of fertilizer of a similar name. 'Anneke' was to be hailed as the most praiseworthy new shrub presented at the Ghent Floralie in the early 1980s.

Breeding for scent resulted in two new cultivars by crossing *Rhododendron luteum* with *R. occidentale*. The association with Ness Gardens had led to a 'production line' of the new seedlings, with Denny doing the crossing and Ness raising thousands of seedlings and rooting cuttings from plants that he could not find space for in his own garden down the road. A well-documented occurrence relates how, one morning, staff found hundreds of cuttings in the propagation unit scattered far and wide across the benches and over the floor. What could have happened? It was quite impossible to accurately reunite each cutting with its proper label, but after reinsertion in the rooting medium, the entire batch was re-labelled 'Blackbird Disturbed'. Consequently, as each new plant came into flower it was given a descriptive note relating to flower colour and origin. Thus, 'Pale Yellow Mr. Pratt' and 'Deep Yellow Mr. Pratt', for example, became common epithets. Denny's cultured sense of humour was delighted by these short phrases, but realising that they would not stand universal approval kept them as sort of private jokes for his many friends.

From this rich vein of new plants came 'Robert Whelan', named for the University's Vice Chancellor, and 'Summer Fragrance'. The former was much admired by all who saw it at the International Garden Festival in

Liverpool in 1984, whilst 'Summer Fragrance' excited tremendous acclaim at the Chelsea Flower Show in 1990. Its subtle fragrance filled the giant marquee and resulted in a frenzy of buying that left the vendor completely out of stock by ten o'clock on the morning of the first day. Significantly, 'Summer Fragrance' extended the flowering season by more than a week, into early June.

This later-flowering characteristic was to have a profound effect on Denny's thinking and resulted in his embarking on a different programme of breeding and selection. He had moved home to Sussex in 1970, following the sudden death of his wife, and having found a property with about one acre of acid soil, he set about developing a garden for his beloved cherries, camellias, magnolias and, of course, rhododendrons. The deciduous rhododendrons finished flowering in mid-June and he considered it would be highly desirable to extend the season. Thus began the work that would consume the rest of his life, to be continued beyond his death by others, and resulting in the establishment of a completely new group, the Ness Holt Hybrids. The naming of these late-June to early-July-flowering azaleas commemorates the Botanic Garden at Ness where Denny found enthusiastic assistance, and his Cheshire home at Ness Holt some ten miles from Chester.

The late-flowering species of deciduous rhododendrons occur naturally in the USA and Denny believed that if he crossed these with some of the best of the hybrid azaleas, he might extend the flowering season beyond June into July or even August. He used *Rhododendron arborescens* with its white, pink-tinged, highly fragrant June flowers; *R. bakeri* with its orange through to crimson-

JOAN WILKINSON

Rhododendron 'Puddington'

red flowers (he used the selection 'Kentucky Colonel'); *R. prunifolium,* especially the cultivar 'Summer Sunset', another July, or even later flowering red; and *R. viscosum* 'Montanum', the delightfully sweet-scented, white-and-pink-flowered Swamp Honey-suckle, as it is known. As a result, he raised thousands of seedlings with the knowledge that he could count on the assistance of Ness Gardens to bring the plants to maturity, and a close friend and neighbour from whom he was able to borrow sufficient additional space to grow them on. The offspring ranged in colour from deep red to pale pink and from orange to pale yellow, one of the best being named by the proprietor of Morrey's Nursery at Kelsall, 'June Fire'. Subsequently, Morrey was to select and name other cultivars, propagating and offering for sale those that held promise, such as 'Denny's Rose', 'Denny's Scarlet' and 'Denny's White'.

Initially only those crosses between *Rhododendron arborescens* and *R. viscosum* had the desired fragrance, but misgivings

'Barnston'	Medium to pale pink.	'Moreton'	Large trusses. White. Best white
'Brimstage'	Medium to pale pink. Good fragrance.	'Ness'	Large flowers. Peachy.
'Burton'	Large flowers. Rose-pink.	'Neston'	Small flowers. Pale pink. Bronze young foliage.
'Denny Pratt'	Large, deep pink – glossy foliage.	'Parkgate'	Pale rose-pink.
'Frankby'	Medium-sized trusses. White.	'Pensby'	Yellow-flushed pink.
'Greasby'	White flushed pink. Very fragrant. Good autumn colour.	'Prenton'	Medium-sized trusses. Deep pink
		'Puddington'	Dense trusses. Pale pink.
'Heswall'	Globular trusses. Yellow. Best yellow.	'Raby'	Pale pink, deeper in bud.
		'Spital'	Large trusses, white.
'Irby'	Pale pink with deeper pink veining.	'Storeton'	Light, clear pink.
'Ledsham'	White flushed pink.	'Thornton Hough'	Pink in bud, opening white.
'Little Neston'	Medium size. Creamy-white.	'Upton'	Deep pink with deeper pink median striping.

NB All the above flowers have an orange or yellow blotching on an upper petal. The degree of fragrance and the intensity of autumn colour is variable but noteworthy.

about colour range, number of flowers per truss and time of flowering led Denny to admit that, *'much remains to be done'*. He determined to use *R. occidentale*, William Lobb's introduction from the Pacific seaboard, to overcome what he perceived as weaknesses. With characteristically large flower trusses this species should, he argued, remedy the defects. Lobb's introduction was the only clone available for breeding to begin with, but as luck would have it, two amateurs, Smith and Mossman, who were looking at populations in northern California, identified no fewer than 270 distinct forms, many of which out classed the original clone.

A few of the best Smith and Mossman clones were used, in particular SM189, resulting in vigorous seedlings varying in size and habit and sometimes producing flower buds in only their second year. These were exciting times, especially waiting to see if the late flowering, fine scent and good autumn colour characteristics had been resolved. Denny wrote in a letter in July 1986,

'I am trying to get the very late flowering Rhododendron serrulatum *from a nursery in South Carolina.'*

His relentless pursuit of new genes was to take him to the bitter end and he died in the winter of 1988 without, as far as is known, employing *R. serrulatum*.

Denny Pratt left unfinished business, and although the breeding work was to die with him, his closest friends were quick to take up the responsibility of ensuring that his plants were not to languish for lack of recognition. The then Director of the University of Liverpool's Botanic Garden, Kenneth Hulme, had been instrumental in encouraging Denny to persevere with his work and determined to bring to Ness as many of the Sussex seedlings as the gardens could accommodate. A well-stocked van load brought over 1,000 seedlings of unknown quality to be planted in the grounds. Others were also to take charge of the Pratt Hybrids, as they were known at that time, and plants found their way to nurseries in Kent and Cheshire as well as to the National Trust property at Dunham Massey on the outskirts of Manchester. A Sussex neighbour, Jack Harrington, to whom Denny had generously presented many seedlings, selected and showed at Vincent Square on the 21 June 1993 two plants: 'Stopham Lass' (now for reasons unknown named 'Stopham Girl') and 'Stopham Lad', the former receiving an Award of Merit when shown to Committee.

Development work now switched to Ness Gardens, where selected clones were planted for public display amongst an already well established and much admired collection of deciduous rhododendrons. The founder of the Gardens in 1898, Arthur Kilpin Bulley, had sponsored some of the 20th century's greatest plant collectors, notably George Forrest and Frank Kingdon Ward, each of whom was responsible for the introduction of new rhododendron species from the Far East.

Although neither had collected in areas rich in deciduous species, Bulley had set out in his private collection some of the early

JOAN WILKINSON

Rhododendron 'Little Neston'

Mollis hybrids in a long border against a hornbeam hedge, a border still in existence today. Some of Denny's very early attempts at hybridisation had been given new planting areas beneath a plantation of North American oak species and it seemed sensible to add to these the 'Pratt Hybrids' of more recent origin. Two such beds were planted with clones that showed particular promise, the criteria for their selection being the three-fold aims of Denny Pratt: late June or July flowering, well-flowered trusses with a fine scent, and good autumn colour.

The site was ideally suited to the establishment of these new clones for, in addition to the late-developing shade of the oaks, the soil was very moisture retentive. Denny said that azaleas needed three things, *water, water and more water*. Politicians do not always have original thoughts!

Most of the thousand or so seedlings brought back to Wirral from Denny's Fittleworth garden in West Sussex were set out in close association in an area of woodland from which further selections could be made. During the 1990s, those of merit were taken and added to the existing populations and a decision was made as to whether they warranted naming and subsequent registration. The choice of cultivar names quickly followed the notion that perhaps 'Pratt Hybrids' had a somewhat unpleasant modern connotation and led to the Ness Holt Hybrid preference. All registered clones were named for Wirral towns or villages with the exception of a wonderful plant, holding many-flowered trusses of rich pink blossoms suffused with orange, held well proud of the glossy foliage; this was named for its raiser, 'Denny Pratt'.

The colours are, it must be said, less vibrant than some of their Knap Hill parents, but this does not detract from their appeal, the softer, less strident pastel shades having a quiet dignity of their own. The dominant hue is pink in all its tints, with 'Neston' bearing exceptional flowers of shell pink lined with deeper pink veining, and 'Ness' carrying flowers of a pale yellow ground colour flushed with the most delicate of pinks and with prominent shrimp pink filaments. The best of the yellow-flowered selections is 'Heswall', its lemon petals enriched by deep butter yellow patches, and the most pleasing

of the white-flowered clones must surely be 'Moreton', not so much for purity of colour but for the contrast of snow white trumpets and the deepest yellow that stains the throat of each.

Would Denny Pratt have approved? Who knows? He would have been delighted, that's for sure, to know that his favourite plants had not died with him but had been carefully nurtured by those who knew and admired him. His willing successors have gladly felt it incumbent upon them to do what they can to ensure the continuation of his legacy. 'Pale Yellow Mr. Pratt' lives on and deserves our recognition.

References

PRATT, M.C. (1977) Breeding Deciduous Azlaeas. *Rhododendrons with Camellias and Magnolias*. Royal Horticultural Society.

PRATT, M.C. (1984/85) Hybrid Deciduous Azaleas. *Rhododendrons with Camellias and Magnolias*. Royal Horticultural Society.

Friends of Ness Garden Newsletter, June 1992. No. 158.

HENDY, J. (1995) Summer Fragrance. *The Garden* Vol.120, Part 5, May 1995. Royal Horticultural Society.

Peter Cunnington is a former curator of Ness Botanic Gardens, the Wirral, Cheshire.

Magnolia Collection of The Scott Arboretum of Swarthmore College

Rhoda Maurer & Eric Hsu

While the Arboretum encompasses more than 300 acres of the Swarthmore College campus, our major collections, consisting of over 2,000 living woody taxa, are concentrated on 110 acres at the heart of the college campus. The Arboretum is a living memorial to Arthur Hoyt Scott (Swarthmore class of 1895), President of the Scott Paper Company and an avid gardener who believed there were too few public gardens for the amateur horticulturist. Through a bequest from Arthur Hoyt Scott's family, the Arboretum was formed in 1929 to display some of the best trees, shrubs, vines and perennials for use in the Delaware Valley.

The Arboretum's collections and gardens are uniquely set amidst a busy college

The magnolia collection at the Scott Arboretum

RHODA MAURER

campus. Swarthmore College is a small, highly selective college of liberal arts and engineering with a student population of approximately 1,300. Founded as a coeducational institution in 1864 by members of the Religious Society of Friends (Quakers), it is nonsectarian but still reflects many Quaker traditions and values. Swarthmore is considered by academicians to be among the best liberal arts colleges in the country.

The Scott Arboretum is located approximately 15 miles southwest of Philadelphia in USDA zone 6B/7A (−15 to −20.5°C). On average, annual rainfall approaches 43in, seasonal snowfall averages just over 20in and the last frost date in spring is approximately 25th April, although it is not uncommon for there to be a devastating frost through 15th May.

The Magnolia Collection

Since the establishment of the Arboretum, the collection has acquired over 487 accessions with 1815 individual plants of the genus *Magnolia*. Currently our collection consists of 212 individuals of 129 taxa with 36 species concentrated in the Magnolia Collection and Tree Peony Garden.

NAPCC (North American Plant Collection Consortium) status was awarded to the Scott Arboretum's Magnolia Collection in September of 2003. This recognition is the second NAPCC collection for the Arboretum as its Holly Collection was awarded in 1995. The NAPCC is a network of North American botanical gardens and arboreta administered by the AABGA (American Association of Botanic Garden and Arboretum) in cooperation with the

Magnolia 'Sunsation'

USDA Agricultural Research Service and the United States National Arboretum. The NAPCC aims to coordinate and improve the collective living plant collections of North America and enhance the conservation and availability of plant germplasm for current and future use.

Within the genus *Magnolia*, the Arboretum's holdings consist of significant collections of *M. × soulangeana* and yellow magnolias, in addition to original distributions of the Little Girl hybrids (*M. stellata* × *M. liliiflora* crosses made by William F. Kosar) introduced by the US National Arboretum. A recent visit by Philippe de Spoelberch (owner of Herkenrode and a Magnolia Society member) in 2003 confirmed that many of the *M. × soulangeana* hybrids that are often confused in the trade are correctly named in the Arboretum's collection. Dr. John C. Wister, the first director of the Arboretum, acquired many of these first additions to the collection from B.H. Slavin, Arthur Slavin, Semmes Nursery, J. Norman Henry, Henry Hicks, Bobbink & Atkins, Tingle Nursery, and Ben Blackburn.

Many of the first yellow hybrids to be introduced to the trade are represented, including *Magnolia* 'Elizabeth' and 'Yellow Bird'. However, many newer introductions have also been consistently acquired through on-going curation of sub-groups, including many of the American hybrids from August Kehr, David Leach and Phil Savage. Through a friendship between Pat McCracken and Ian Simpkins (curatorial intern 1997–1998), the Arboretum acquired the following yellow hybrids: 'Hot Flash', 'Tranquility', 'Solar Flair', 'Sunburst', 'Gold Crown', 'Golden Endeavor', 'Gold Cup', and

RHODA MAURER

Magnolia 'Betty'

RHODA MAURER

'Stellar Acclaim'. More recent Brooklyn Botanic Garden introductions, 'Lois', 'Hattie Carthan' and 'Judy Zuk' (BBGRC 1164), are also included in the collection. While the majority of the yellow magnolias have yet to reach their mature sizes, several, particularly 'Sundance', 'Sunsation' (see picture, opposite), and 'Legend' already show the potential to become large trees (a trait likely inherited from *M. acuminata* background). The yellow colouring of the flowers has proved elusive since they tend towards creamy yellow, although 'Gold Crown', 'Judy Zuk', and 'Yellow Bird' possess that desirable deep yellow hue. Nonetheless, young trees flower generously at a precocious age; 'Golden Gift' bears prolific flowers throughout the branches. A Brooklyn Botanic Garden introduction whose name honors the recently retired President of Brooklyn Botanic Garden, 'Judy Zuk' promises to assume a fastigiate habit rather than the broad spread of other yellow magnolias; the chalice shape and the deep yellow flushed pink color of the fruity fragranced flowers adds further appeal to this recently named hybrid.

Several *Magnolia denudata* in the Arboretum's collection have a distinctive fastigiate habit that was noted by John Hillier during his last visit to Philadelphia in 2003.

One plant near Bond Quad in particular has caught both his and Pat McCracken's attention; this selection with its very columnar habit is worth introducing and naming as it may be an excellent magnolia for small gardens.

The Little Girl hybrids at the Arboretum consist of *Magnolia* 'Ann', 'Betty' (see picture, above), 'Jane', 'Judy', 'Pinkie', 'Ricki', and 'Susan', a complete selection except for 'Randy' (this cultivar was unfortunately removed as part of new construction on campus). Apart from small plants of 'Judy' and 'Ricki' in the growing area, all of these US National Arboretum introductions have proved to be multi-stemmed, round shrubby trees that have magnificent floral display, followed by sporadic flowers in late summer to early autumn. They generally escape the late spring frosts that decimate the early-flowering magnolias in our collection.

In addition to hybrids, the Arboretum has been steadily building up its collection of American species, which include *Magnolia*

Magnolia stellata 'Centennial', showing flower detail (inset)

RHODA MAURER

acuminata, *M. ashei*, *M. cordata*, *M. fraseri*, *M. grandiflora*, *M. macrophylla*, *M. pyramidata*, *M. tripetala*, and *M. virginiana*. These species have proved amenable to cultivation here, taking the hot summers and cold winters in their stride. *M. virginiana* is well represented by several cultivars, one of which had its origins at the Arboretum. Dr Wister had acquired many magnolias from Henry Hicks of Hicks Nursery in Westbury, New York. During the Magnolia Society's visit in 1971, one particular *M. virginiana* received in 1937 caused quite a stir. This evergreen specimen was later introduced by the Scott Arboretum as *M. virginiana* var. *australis* 'Henry Hicks'; the type specimen still resides in the Magnolia Collection.

However, another specimen of 'Henry Hicks' in the Entrance Garden has not retained its evergreen characteristic, and rather assumed a semi-deciduous one that requires constant clean-up of shed leaves and branches throughout the year. Its tendency to shed leaves may be a result of rootstock influence on the graft. *M. virginiana* var. *australis* 'Henry Hicks' is unfortunately difficult to propagate from cuttings and therefore must be grafted. Another cultivar, *M. virginiana* 'Santa Rosa', planted in the courtyard of the college's chimes tower, Clothier Hall, has proven to be a vigorous grower (20ft tall) with handsome lustrous, evergreen leaves. It has developed an upright leader with a branching habit. *M. virginiana* 'Satellite', which has been slow-growing to date (5ft tall), is a US National Arboretum introduction and has prominent blue-grey leaf undersides and creamy white flowers 3in across. Along with *M. grandiflora*, *M. virginiana* often marks the seasonal finale to the main magnolia display during spring.

Goals for the Collection and Future Plans
Through institutional and staff dedication and collaborations, the Arboretum has been able to continually diversify its collection over the years. The Arboretum hopes to represent superior specimens including those with best flower color, frost tolerance, and later bloom time suited for the climate of the Delaware Valley while focusing on yellow hybrids, saucer magnolias, significant selection of species and American natives. Ultimately the Arboretum anticipates holding 250 taxa with final numbers only dependent upon

List of Magnolia Taxa at the Scott Arboretum of Swarthmore College as of 12th August 2005		
M. acuminata	M. x kewensis 'Wada's	M. x soulangeana
M. 'Ann'	Memory'	'Lombardy Rose'
M. ashei	M. kobus	M. x soulangeana 'Norbertii'
M. 'Betty'	M. kobus var. borealis	M. x soulangeana 'Rustica
M. x brooklynensis 'Hattie	M. 'Legend'	Rubra'
Carthan'	M. x loebneri 'Ballerina'	M. sp.
M. 'Butterflies'	M. x loebneri 'Leonard Messel'	M. 'Spectrum'
M. 'Candy Cane'	M. x loebneri 'Merrill'	M. sprengeri var. diva 'Diva'
M. 'Charles Coates'	M. x loebneri 'Neil McEachern'	M. 'Star Wars'
M. cordata	M. x loebneri 'Super Star'	M. 'Stellar Acclaim'
M. cylindrica	M. x loebneri 'Vegetable	M. stellata
M. 'Daybreak'	Garden'	M. stellata 'Centennial'
M. denudata	M. x loebneri 'Willowwood'	M. stellata 'Rosea'
M. 'Elizabeth'	M. macrophylla	M. stellata 'Royal Star'
M. 'Firefly'	M. macrophylla x tripetala	M. stellata 'Waterlily'
M. 'Galaxy'	M. 'Marillyn'	M. 'Sundance'
M. 'Gold Crown'	M. 'Maxine Merrill'	M. 'Sunsation'
M. 'Gold Star'	M. officinalis	M. 'Sunspire'
M. 'Golden Endeavor'	M. officinalis var. biloba	M. 'Susan'
M. 'Golden Gift'	M. 'Paul Cook'	M. tripetala
M. grandiflora	M. 'Royal Crown'	M. x veitchii
M. grandiflora 'Bracken's	M. salicifolia	M. virginiana
Brown Beauty'	M. sieboldii	M. virginiana var. australis
M. grandiflora 'D.D.	M. 'Slavin's Snowy'	'Henry Hicks'
Blanchard'	M. 'Solar Flair'	M. virginiana var. australis
M. grandiflora 'Edith Bogue'	M. x soulangeana	'Milton'
M. grandiflora 'Hasse'	M. x soulangeana 'Alba	M. virginiana 'Cully'
M. grandiflora 'Victoria'	Superba'	M. virginiana 'Santa Rosa'
M. 'Hot Flash'	M. x soulangeana	M. 'Vulcan'
M. 'Ivory Chalice'	'Alexandrina'	M. 'Woodsman'
M. 'Jon Jon'	M. x soulangeana 'Amabilis'	M. 'Yellow Lantern'
M. 'Judy Zuk'	M. x soulangeana 'Brozzonii'	M. zenii

space limitations. The Arboretum has an open policy for botanical gardens and nurseries with permission to propagate holdings in hope that its collections will serve as a germplasm for other collections. It is also hoped that other important collections are awarded NAPCC status and that collaborations are established to ensure breadth in holdings of the genus *Magnolia* across the country.

To accomplish these goals, the Arboretum plans to curate sub-groups of the collection on a rotational basis. Currently curation of exotic species of the genus and selections of *Magnolia stellata, M. kobus* and *M. × loebneri* will be evaluated with a re-evaluation of the saucer magnolias due by the end of 2005. During 2005–2006, a re-assessment of the yellow hybrids and other August Kehr hybrids will be completed. In 2006–2007, a re-assessment of the American natives will be conducted. Additionally, new planting ground has been designated by the Collection's Committee for expansion of the collection.

Digital images of each specimen in the collection will be linked to the plant records database for documentation and educational purposes. An earnest effort to photograph this past spring's display was conducted with the assistance of one full-time staff member and four volunteers. Collecting digital images of this and other prominent collections will continue. Plant records information is currently posted on the web through our website www.scottarboretum.org and through the BG-BASE multi-institution website rbg-web2.rbge.org.uk/forms/multisite2.html hosted by the Royal Botanic Garden Edinburgh, making our taxa list available to a broader range of professionals.

Currently, we are reviewing our collections page and making improvements to the depth of information and ease of access.

To reach amateur gardeners with information about the collection, the Arboretum conducts workshops on specific genera. Well-attended seasonal tours led by staff members in April and May focus on the Magnolia and Cherry Collections. A feature on our collection appeared on Martha Stewart Living in May 2003. Articles continue to be published about our collections in horticultural magazines and journals. Free brochures provided to visitors are updated every winter and immediate goals include adding computer generated maps. This autumn, the Arboretum plans to expand our interpretation center with a visitor's computer station where searchable plant records data and hardiness information will be available; visitors will also be able to create and print customised maps, digital images and featured tours.

The Arboretum is dedicated to continued staff involvement with the International Magnolia Society both locally and internationally since it became a member in 1963. Current Arboretum staff members have attended Magnolia Society meetings in Italy, New Zealand and South Korea. In 2004, the Arboretum hosted the Society during their visit to Philadelphia in late May (a trip focusing on American natives). We also hope to send a representative to the 2006 Magnolia Society meeting in Japan.

Rhoda Maurer is the Plants Records Supervisor and Eric Hsu a Curatorial Intern, both at The Scott Arboretum of Swarthmore College, Swarthmore, Philadelphia PA 19081, USA

HANS ROBENEK AND HIS RHODODENDRONS

❦

GERALD DIXON

Hans Robenek

Although most rhododendron collections hold at least one of this breeder's hybrids, the scope of his work is little known in the UK. Hans Robenek was fortunate enough to be able to spend his whole working life dealing with these wonderful plants and his knowledge of their development in continental Europe over the last 50 years was second to none.

Born in 1920 in the German part of what is now Czechoslovakia, Hans served an apprenticeship as a gardener until being drafted for military service in World War Two.

At the end of the war he found himself recovering from his wounds in a hospital in Westerstede, a town in the heart of what subsequently became the main growing area for rhododendrons in Europe. As luck would have it, a local farmer called Dietrich Hobbie was looking for a trained gardener to act as foreman in his newly-formed rhododendron nursery.

During the 1930s Hobbie had become fascinated with these plants and had regularly received wild-collected seeds, from, amongst others, Sir William Wright Smith of Edinburgh Botanic Gardens. These included many introductions of the Ludlow and Sheriff and Professor Hu expeditions. Throughout the war Hobbie had been looking after the small seedlings more or less single-handed and now needed professional help in dealing with them.

The first task Hans Robenek was given was to transplant the thousands of species seedlings into beds in Hobbie's woodland. His intimate knowledge of more than 100 species was formed in this period and was to develop over the next six decades. Propagation in those days was in its infancy and it was Hans Robenek who introduced the process of grafting to the Hobbie nursery, first using *Rhododendron catawbiense* seedlings as an understock and later the more reliable and now standard practice of using rooted cuttings of 'Cunningham's White'.

By the late 1940s Hobbie had flowered many of his successful *Rhododenron repens* and *williamsianum* hybrids and he actively encouraged his head gardener, foreman and right-hand man to follow his own independent breeding program. There was a friendly rivalry and often differing opinions on choice of parentage, Hobbie preferring to make use of the grex concept where he could remake successful crosses, producing large numbers of saleable seedlings of similar characteristics. Hans Robenek was more interested in producing unusual colour combinations, not aiming at the mass market but at the private enthusiast.

A good example of this was his use of *Rhododendron viscidifolium*. Grown as a seedling from the 1938 expedition of Ludlow, Sherriff and Taylor, this first flowered in the Hobbie Park around 1950. Hobbie himself wasn't keen on its strong colour and somewhat miffy constitution, being more interested in producing lighter creams and yellows, based on the many available and robust *R. campylocarpum* hybrids. Hans Robenek, however, saw the potential for producing a hardy yellow much deeper in tone than at that time available. He crossed *R. viscidifolium* with *R. orbiculare, R. metternichii,* 'Catalgla', *R. wardii,* 'Doctor

V.H. Rutgers' and 'Adriaan Koster'; this last cross producing the well-known 'Viscy'.

He made many other crosses over the 40 years he spent with Hobbie, often using species like *Rhododendron insigne* as the seed-bearer to provide hardiness and some of the less-hardy hybrids like 'Goldsworth Orange' to introduce colour. Similar to Hobbie, he preferred to use at least one species in his crosses but often tended to use more complex hybrids as the seed-bearer.

Hans retired in 1984 at the age of 65 after working nearly 40 years with Dietrich Hobbie. Together with a handful of workers, he had created what is surely the most beautiful rhododendron park on the continent. Over this long period he was solely responsible for the daily running of the nursery and, after his early morning meeting with Dietrich Hobbie, he would oversee the tasks they had planned for that day.

The death of Dietrich Hobbie in 1985 marked the end of a wonderful era in which the partnership of these two men had completely changed the face of gardening in Germany. Anyone who has witnessed the town of Westerstede during Rhododendron Week will appreciate the long-lasting effect of their influence.

After his own retirement and the death of his friend and mentor, Hans never again entered the park they had created together, preferring to leave its future to the new generation.

For the five years previous to his leaving Hobbie, he had started to build up his own small nursery and was now, with the help of his wife Anna, able to concentrate on further evaluating his own crosses. Many of the hybrids produced during his time with Hobbie had already been introduced and in 1990 he registered a further 20 varieties.

His nursery became well known among rhododendron buffs, in particular for his collection of species. Many of these originated from seeds provided by Edinburgh and represented possibly the hardiest selection of species available in Europe. He took great pride in conserving these varieties in the knowledge that although they may not have been 'typical' in today's sense, they were robust and hardy.

The following descriptions of his hybrids are based on their performance in our east Devon nursery: Most have been formally registered, some of them very recently.

'Anna Robenek' ((*fortunei* subsp. *discolor* × 'Catharine van Tol') × 'Goldsworth Orange')
Flat-topped trusses of up to 21 funnel-shaped flowers, on the outside in bright purplish red, inside a lighter purplish-rose becoming still lighter towards the center. The dorsal lobes hold strong dark-red markings. A medium-sized bush which prefers a little shade. Named by the breeder for his wife Anna. May-June

'Calotray' (*calophytum* × *traillianum*)
Close flat-topped trusses of creamy white with red markings. A beautiful foliage plant with leaves similar to calophytum but with the indumentum and growth habit of traillianum. Free flowering once established. April.

'Doctor Frank Robenek' ('Francis Hanger' hybrid)
Double orange-red flowers with a large flared calyx. Relatively slow-growing and very

tough. A beautiful plant when in full flower but doesn't like too much sun. Named for his son Frank. May-June.

'Dugerald' (*wardii* × *viscidifolium*)
Lax trusses of golden-yellow trumpet-shaped flowers on a compact and slow-growing, somewhat twiggy bush. This variety, considered a collectors' item by many was never really hardy enough for the German climate but thrives in the UK. May.

'Elfenbein' ('Adriaan Koster' × *williamsianum*)
A sister-seedling of Gartendirektor Rieger. Slightly smaller flowers but of a deeper shade of cream. Very tough with a compact habit. April-May.

'Elke Robenek' ('Goldsworth Orange' × ('John Walter' × *dichroanthum* subsp. *scyphocalyx*))
Flat-topped trusses of multicoloured flowers, cherry-red outside, yellow inside with rose edging. Light-green foliage on an upright bush. Appreciates some shade and likes to be well fed. Possibly the most colourful of his hybrids and a favorite with many. Named for his daughter. May-June.

'Feuersturm' ((*insigne* × 'Goldsworth Orange') × 'Thunderstorm')
Red buds opening to fiery red flowers with an orange throat. Very popular and effective when in full flower. May-June.

'Fruehlingsleuchten'
('Metternianum' × 'Soulkew')
Perfectly rounded trusses of large, pure white bowl-shaped flowers on a low-growing sturdy bush. Similar in many ways to 'Seven Stars' but much hardier and more robust. May.

65

'Fuego' ('Madame de Bruin' × *haematodes*)
Open trusses of shining red hanging flowers on a low-growing, compact bush. Possibly the breeder's best red hybrid and very popular. May-June.

'Gardon' (*decorum* × *wardii* var. *puralbum*)
This beautifully scented pure white variety produces abundant flowers in a lovely rounded truss. The growth is compact with very attractive dark-green foliage. Named for his grandson. May.

'Gartendirektor Rieger' ('Adriaan Koster' × *williamsianum*)
Large creamy-white flowers with red markings on a compact, rounded bush. Very tough with beautiful shiny, rugose foliage. This, together with Viscy, is the most well-known of his hybrids. Very reliable and free flowering. April-May.

'Georg Robenek' ('Mrs Lindsay Smith' × 'Orange Favorit')
Close trusses of light-red flowers with a yellow throat, the red more pronounced on the outer veins and with copious red spots. A compact bush with attractive narrow foliage. Named for his son Georg. May.

'Geske' (*orbiculare* × *viscidifolium*)
Lax trusses of beautiful open-faced flowers in an unusual matt-red/orange tone. This hybrid has the somewhat twiggy growth of most viscidifolium hybrids, producing a delicate rounded shrub of perfect balance. Named for his youngest granddaughter. May.

'Goldglanz' (('Goldsworth Orange' × 'Insigne') × 'Goldsworth Orange'))
Flat-topped trusses of light-yellow flowers flushed orange with a prominent winged calyx. A beautiful colour-combination with attractive narrow foliage on a dense-growing compact bush. June.

'Helgoland' ('Scandinavia' × *yakushimanum*)
Flowers of intense rose with yellowish markings. Compact growth. May-June.

'Hultschin' (*insigne* × *williamsianum*)
Compact trusses of light rose flowers on a close-growing bush. Attractive foliage and free-flowering once established. May.

'Lavendelzauber'
('Purple Splendour' × *yakushimanum*)
Close rounded trusses on wavy-edged flowers in a delicate lilac tone. Good shiny foliage on a very low-growing bush. May.

'Ludgerstal' (('John Walter' × *fortunei* subsp. *discolor*) × 'Goldsworth Orange')
Perfectly-shaped round trusses of funnel-shaped flowers in dark-rose, lighter around the midribs and with dark-red spotting on an orange background. Compact, wide growth and free-flowering once established. June.

'Maizauber' (*traillianum* × *williamsianum*)
Large brown flower-buds open an intense pink, fading gradually through a clear light rose and finally becoming pure white. Very attractive ovate foliage on a compact bush. April.

'Manon Robenek' (*fortunei* subsp. *discolor* hybrid × *dichroanthum* subsp. *scyphocalyx*)
Elegant loose trusses of large funnel shaped flowers in yellow-orange with red edging to the lobes. A compact bush with interesting upcurved foliage. Named for his granddaughter. May.

'**Milka**' ('Goldsworth Orange' × ('John Walter' × *dichroanthum* subsp. *scyphocalyx*))
Lax trusses of open-faced orange-rose flowers fading to yellow on the inside and with a darker throat. Neat foliage on a compact medium-growing bush. Named by the breeder in honour of his mother. May-June.

'**Napoli**' ('Goldsworth Orange' hybrid × *dichroanthum* subsp. *scyphocalyx*)
Compact trusses of orange-yellow open faced flowers with rose edging. Very compact and low-growing. May.

'**Petersfeld**' (*wardii* × 'Goldsworth Orange')
Neat trusses of yellow and orange flowers on a compact, low-growing bush. One of Hans Robenek's best yellows. June.

'**Prinz Karneval**' ('Louis Pasteur' × 'Goldsworth Orange')
An unusual two-tone combination with the outside of the flowers light-red and the inside white with red edging to the lobes. Good contrast on a wide-growing bush. May-June.

'**Professor Horst Robenek**' ('Germania' × 'Antoon van Welie')
Giant matt-green buds opening to rose-red wavy flowers in tight trusses. Very floriferous, even as a small plant. Neat foliage on a close, compact bush. Named by the breeder for his eldest son. May.

'**Ratibor**' (*insigne* × *forrestii* Repens Group)
Open trusses in rose-red on a medium sized shrub with insigne-type foliage. Very close-growing. April-May.

'**Rexima**' (*yakushimanum* × *rex*)
Flowers fading to white with a dark-red basal flare. Foliage similar to *rex* but with the indumentum of *yakushimanum*. May.

'**Rixte**' ('Goldsworth Orange' × *insigne*)
Delicate pastel shades of light orange and pink, held in elegant flat-topped trusses. Neat foliage on a compact, low-growing bush. Named for his granddaughter. June.

'**Robenek's Inamorata**' (*fortunei* subsp. *discolor* × *wardii*)
Large creamy yellow open-faced flowers with a bright-red flare in the throat, held in a lax truss of about 8. Medium growth on an upright bush. June

Rosenkoenigen (*souliei* hybrid × 'Soulkew')
Large trusses of up to 17 bowl-shaped flowers, the reverse in light purplish-pink the inside a lilac-pink lightening to near white at the centre, with a heavy black-red basal flare. Compact and hardy. May-June.

'**Silberfee**' ('Mrs Lindsay Smith' × *yakushimanum*)
Rounded trusses in clear white with faint yellow markings. Low-growing and free flowering. May.

'**Silja**' ('Doctor V.H. Rutgers' × *viscidifolium*)
Lax trusses of orange-red trumpet-shaped flowers on a rounded bush. Very slender, twiggy growth adding to the effect of lightness and delicacy. April-May.

'**Soft Satin**' ('Hultschin' × *yakushimanum*)
White flowers with frilled edging of delicate lilac. Compact. May.

'Spring Sun'
('Adriaan Koster' × *williamsianum*)
Another sister seedling of 'Gartendirektor Rieger'. Similar in tone to 'Elfenbein' but with a pronounced basal blotch. April-May.

'Tropau' (*dichroanthum* subsp. *scyphocalyx* hybrid × *yakushimanum*)
Neat trusses of white flowers with rose margins and green spots. May.

'Viscy' ('Diane' × *viscidifolium*)
Heavy-textured whisky-coloured flowers with red spotting which is held over a longer flowering period than most hybrids. Makes a very compact, wide-growing bush with beautiful shiny foliage. This is easily the most widely-grown of Hans Robenek's hybrids and is very effective in an open position where the beautiful habit can develop freely. May.

'Walter Schmalscheidt' (*wardii* × 'Linsweger Gold')
Open trusses of saucer-shaped flowers in clear yellow. Similar in growth to *R. wardii* but much more compact. Needs a little shade to perform at its best but very beautiful when well-grown. May.

'Zigeunerin' ('Louis Pasteur' × 'Goldsworth Orange')
Outside and inner-edge of flower light-red, inside fading to white. A very distinctive colour contrast on a wide-growing bush. May-June.

'Zugspitze'
(*puralbum* hybrid × *yakushimanum*)
Bell-shaped flowers of purest white on a low-growing bush. One of our favourite *yakushimanum* hybrids and very popular. May.

Hans Robenek passed away in February 2005 after a short illness. His widow Anna, his five children and many of his twelve grandchildren, all of whom he was immensely proud, are now very busy transforming the nursery into a wonderful private park, providing a suitable setting for the many hybrids this great gardener had produced.

A modest and unassuming man, our friend and travelling companion of over 25 years, Hans Robenek will be sorely missed by all who knew him.

Many of his hybrids are featured in our catalogue and can be ordered from our nursery. The remaining more recent ones are presently being propagated and will be made available over the next few years.

Gerald Dixon is a member of the Group and is the founder of Brooklands Nurseries at Shute near Axminster in Devon

RICHARD B. FIGLAR

A New Classification for *Magnolia*

Botanical classification is the result of the arranging of individual plants into logical groupings based on genetic closeness (evolutionary history or phylogeny), naming those entities (using the Linnaean system), then by application of similar scientific criteria, placing those groups into larger groups and so on and so forth. For well over 200 years, taxonomists have relied almost entirely on morphological observations, often of herbarium specimens, to develop classifications. The process is far from perfect. After all, what constitutes a character? What constitutes a meaningful change in that character, and how does the observer determine whether the character is taxonomically important or simply a result of parallel evolution? No doubt, speculation is involved. The Lord Aberconway aptly reminded us of this when he was introducing James E. Dandy to an RHS Camellia and Magnolia Conference discussion session in 1950, "All classifications have the defects of their virtues, and the best of them have the virtues of their defects."

With his 1927 publication of "The Genera of Magnolieae," James E. Dandy introduced a system of classification for tribe Magnolieae (referred to here as subfamily Magnolioideae) that was to be essentially unchallenged for the next 51 years. [He excluded from the discussion, *Liriodendron,*

the obviously distinct genus of the other subfamily or tribe in Magnoliaceae.] Prior to that time with up to 10 genera described, there had been a fair amount of contention among botanists regarding Magnolioideae systematics. Bentham and Hooker (1862) recognised just four genera: *Talauma, Magnolia, Manglietia* and *Michelia*; Prantl (1888) reduced the number of genera to 3 by reduction of *Manglietia* to *Magnolia*; while Ballion (1866) immersed all into *Magnolia*. According to Dandy (1927), Ballion had suggested that all genera should be described as subgenera of one genus, *Magnolia*, or keep all 10 genera and thus allow for the creation of additional genera by circumstance "of single and unimportant characters." Ballion chose the former, and in 1927 Dandy chose the latter, although at the time he hadn't realised it.

In creating his 1927 classification, Dandy evidently put considerable weight on four characters: the position of the flower (axillary or terminal), the number of ovules per carpel, type of fruit (free longitudinally dehiscent carpels vs. concrescent circumscissile carpels), and the presence or absence of a gynophore (a stalk between the androecium and gynoecium on the floral axis). This allowed him to uphold Bentham & Hooker's system of *Magnolia* (terminal flowers, 2 ovules per carpel, free carpels / longitudinally dehiscent, and no gynophore), *Talauma* (concrescent carpels/circumscissile), *Manglietia* (4 or more ovules per carpel), and *Michelia* (axillary flowers, gynophore). At the same time it also permitted him to uphold or create smaller "splinter" genera. Accordingly, he was able to separate *Elmerrillia* (axillary flowers, no gynophore) and *Alcimandra* (terminal flowers, gynophore) from *Michelia* (axillary flowers, gynophore). He also separated Blume's genus (1825), *Aromadendron* ("indehiscent" fleshy fruit), from *Talauma* and then added his two newly described species as two new genera: *Pachylarnax* ("capsular" concrescent fruit) and *Kmeria* (ventrally dehiscent carpels, unisexual flowers), in the latter case obviously putting significance to unisexual flowers as well.

Dandy eventually subdivided genus *Magnolia* into the familiar 2 subgenera, *Magnolia* (with sections *Magnolia, Gwillimia, Lirianthe, Rhytidospermum, Oyama, Theorhodon, Gynopodium,* and *Maingola*) and *Yulania* (with sections *Yulania, Buergeria,* and *Tulipastrum*). See Dandy (1978), and a graphic representation in Kim *et al.* (2001a).

Dandy's classification not only survived unchallenged for over half a century, it served as a "template" for other botanists to create even more splinter genera often by using different combinations of Dandy's 4 or 5 character states, in a way, just as Baillon had predicted. For example, in 1940 a Chinese botanist, H.H. Hu, described the new monotypic genus, *Paramichelia*, to account for the *Aromadendron*-like fruits of this otherwise *Michelia*-like taxon. Hu and a co-author Cheng (1951b) even concocted genus *Paramanglietia* to accommodate a perceived variation in the fruiting character in what

others recognised as *Manglietia aromatica.* Fortunately in this case, few, if any, botanists ever recognised genus *Paramanglietia.*

Hu and Cheng (1951a) would also create the genus *Parakmeria* to replace Dandy's *Magnolia* section *Gynopodium* to account for the incidence of only male flowers on some trees of species of this section. Though their reasoning seemed to be concordant with Dandy's template involving unisexual flowers and generic separation (as the name *Parakmeria* implies, "near" *Kmeria,* the genus with unisexual flowers), Dandy apparently never accepted this, nor, to my knowledge, had he ever commented on it. It's possible that he was unaware of it, as information from China wasn't widely available to Western botanists at that time. Dandy did accept another genus built on his template: *Tsoongiodendron,* a monotypic genus described by Chun Woon-Young in 1963 based on its *Talauma*-like fruits on an otherwise *Michelia*-like taxon.

Around that same time Liu Yu-Hu (Law Yuh-Wu) was gaining prominence in China as a leading Magnoliaceae botanist and taxonomist. He would embrace the Dandy template including the splinter genera *Paramichelia, Parakmeria, Tsoongiodendron,* and even added one of his own in 1979, *Manglietiastrum,* another monotypic genus based on relatively subtle differences in its fruit (from that of *Pachylarnax*). He also tinkered with his system by collecting the various genera into seemingly superfluous groups of tribes and subtribes to account for the now larger number of "genera" with common characters, such as axillary flowers etc. (Law, 1984 & 1996).

Some challenge to Dandy's system did begin to materialise in the late 1970s. Hsuan

Keng, a botany professor at the University of Singapore, concluded that *Manglietia, Talauma,* and *Aromadendron* should be merged with *Magnolia* since the only thing separating them were slight differences in fruit (Keng, 1978). Moreover, he regarded the weakest genus as *Manglietia,* since *Magnolia* includes some taxa with 4-ovulate carpels as in *Manglietia.* His reduction received little attention, however, possibly because the journal in which it was published was not widely circulated.

Finally in the early 1980s, Hans P. Nooteboom, of the then Rijksherbarium at Leiden University in The Netherlands, took up the revision of Magnoliaceae for *Flora Malesiana* after the original author, James E. Dandy, died and left an unpublished manuscript. The huge variability of the tropical species made Dandy uncertain about the circumscription of species. That resulted in his never publishing his treatments. Nooteboom studied Dandy's vouchers, which were still intact after Dandy's death in 1978, and spent months studying Magnoliaceae throughout the Malesian Archipelago. Nooteboom made a stunning finding: concrescent carpels are essentially the same morphological expression as free carpels, except that in concrescent fruits, it's this fusion of the outer parts of the mesocarp that is responsible for their mainly circumscissile dehiscence. He also discovered that concrescent fruits of some *Talauma* spp., and *Tsoongiodendron* actually employ both modes (longitudinal and circumscissile) of dehiscence, thus giving the appearance of typical *Magnolia* fruit. He went on to say that concrescence of carpels probably evolved separately in the various lineages. [This "intermediate" form of fruit dehiscence was also recognised in *Magnolia cylindrica* by Stephen Spongberg (1998). See also Figlar (2002a) and Holliger (2003).]

On these grounds, Nooteboom (1985) reduced *Talauma,* (including a similar South American genus, *Dugandiodendron*), *Aromadendron,* and Liu's *Manglietiastrum* to *Magnolia,* and using the same argument, two splinter genera, *Tsoongiodendron* and *Paramichelia,* were reduced to *Michelia.* Perhaps feeling that he had taken on enough at this point, Nooteboom didn't sufficiently challenge Dandy's other three characters: flower position, gynophore presence, and ovules per carpel. So, *Michelia* and *Manglietia* remained intact, but Dandy's monotypic splinter genus, *Alcimandra,* was reduced to *Magnolia* based on its overall similarity to section *Gynopodium.*

In the early 1990s new science began to have impacts on the system of Magnoliaceae, especially the use of molecular (DNA) sequence data to examine taxonomic relationships. DNA has several obvious advantages over traditional morphological characters. DNA sequences provide far more characters, usually in the thousands, than can be found by morphological observation. More importantly, DNA characters don't require the subjective (and often speculative) assessment of the human observer. Using computers to compare corresponding sets of base pair sequences for each species sampled, phylogenetic trees or cladograms are constructed. Heuristics are then used to select the most optimal trees, and modern statistical methods are employed to evaluate reliability of the results. Theoretically, then, it is possible that a tree can represent the true phylogenic relationship for a given set of organisms (Kumar & Filipski, 2001).

One of the first meaningful DNA analyses using Magnoliaceae taxa (Qiu, 1993) revealed that the American *Magnolia tripetala* was not closely related to *M. macrophylla,* or *M. fraseri* as had been previously thought. Instead, it formed a tight clade with the Asian *Rhytidospermum.* Additional work by Qiu, then joined by Parks and Chase (1995a, 1995b), not only confirmed that relationship, but the new cladogram also showed *Manglietia* and *Michelia* both nested within *Magnolia.*

Taking note of these new findings, I began a morphological study of Magnoliaceae taxa, but instead of relying mostly on herbarium specimens, I concentrated on observing live plants. I found several characters that *Magnolia* subgenus *Yulania* spp. had in common with *Michelia* spp., but were not present in *Magnolia* subgenus *Magnolia* spp. The evidence was compelling: both (*Michelia* and subg. *Yulania*) produce branches by prolepsis (from buds of previous year's growth), bloom precociously in early spring before new leaves appear, and produce pseudo-axillary flowers (actually terminal on abbreviated branchlets), more so in *Michelia* spp., less so in subg. *Yulania*. In contrast, subg. *Magnolia* has sylleptic branching (branches produced from buds on current year's growth), blooms later in the season after new leaves appear, and those blooms are always terminal on typical shoots. With encouragement from Hans Nooteboom and Stephen Spongberg, I presented my findings and subsequent reduction of *Michelia* and *Elmerrillia* to *Magnolia* at the International Symposium on the Family Magnoliaceae at Guangzhou China in 1998 (Figlar, 2000).

At the ISFM conference, independent DNA studies of Magnoliaceae by teams headed by Kunihiko Ueda (Ueda *et al.,* 2000), Sangtae Kim (Kim *et al.,* 1998), and Hiroshi Azuma (Azuma *et al.,* 2000) were presented. As could be expected, all three produced essentially the same phylogenetic tree: *Manglietia* is nested within subgenus *Magnolia,* and *Michelia* is nested within *Magnolia* as sister (forming a larger clade) to subgenus *Yulania.* It was noteworthy that these DNA results and my morphological findings were mutually supportive.

These and other important findings presented at the ISFM conference served as a springboard for more intensive taxonomic research using both DNA and morphology. Sangtae Kim and his team went on to build a more ambitious DNA analysis using *ndhF* sequences of 99 taxa representing essentially all of the (perceived) Magnoliaceae lineages. [Many of us contributed specimens of Magnoliaceae taxa for this effort including John T. Gallagher of the RHS.] Kim's landmark study was published as the cover story in American Journal of Botany (Kim *et al.* 2001a). The result yielded a most parsimonious phylogenetic tree containing 11 strongly supported clades (see Figure 1, opposite). Major findings include:

• The *Michelia* clade (Clade 1) associates with the subgenus *Yulania* clade (Clade 2) as in previous DNA studies, but this time the newly added taxa represented by lineages, *Elmerrillia, Aromadendron,* and *Magnolia* sections *Alcimandra* & *Maingola* are all positioned within the *Michelia* clade (including the former splinter genera *Tsoongiodendron* and *Paramichelia*).

- Section *Gynopodium* forms a well-supported Clade 3, which includes *Pachylarnax* and Liu's *Manglietiastrum*. Clade 3 is closely associated with the Clades 1 and 2, and altogether they form a single larger clade of moderate support.
- *Magnolia virginiana* (section *Magnolia*) is placed clearly within the section *Theorhodon* (Clade 4).
- Sections *Gwillimia*, *Lirianthe*, and *Blumiana* (the first two of *Magnolia*, the last one of the former Asian *Talauma*) form one affiliation as Clade 6.
- Section *Rhytidospermum* (excluding *M. macrophylla*, *M. fraseri* and their varieties) and section *Oyama* each form strongly supported clades, but together the two sections form a larger strongly supported Clade 9.
- Five additional, well supported clades are represented by each of: *Kmeria* (Clade 5), *M. macrophylla* and its

varieties (Clade 11), *M. fraseri* and its var. *pyramidata* (Clade 10), *Manglietia* (Clade 8), and the tropical American lineages represented by the former genera *Talauma* and *Dugandiodendron*, and section *Splendentes* of *Magnolia* (Clade 7).

Thus, on the surface, it looked as if genus *Magnolia* could be simplified into just 11 groups or sections. Kim *et al.* (2001b) later replicated this study using more data from multiple genes (9000 base pairs). The results were even more convincing. Bootstrap values, statistics that measure reliability of clades, for each of the 11 clades ranged from 82 to 100 (7 clades had 100, the maximum). Curiously, the multiple gene data did not significantly improve phylogenetic resolution of the relationships between clades, particularly the basal 8. So the evolutionary order (from most primitive at the base to most derived at the top) of those 8 clades was still unclear.

Clade Number	Constituent Lineages (using nomenclature of Dandy (1978), Nooteboom (1985), or Liu (1984) for illustrative purposes).
Clade 1	*Michelia* (including *Tsoongiodendron* and *Paramichelia*), *Elmerrillia*, *Aromadendron*, *Magnolia* sections *Alcimandra* and *Maingola*.
Clade 2	*Magnolia* subgenus *Yulania*.
Clade 3	*Magnolia* subgenus *Gynopodium*, *Pachylarnax*, and *Manglietiastrum*.
Clade 4	*Magnolia* sections *Magnolia* and *Theorhodon*.
Clade 5	*Kmeria*
Clade 6	Sections *Gwillimia*, *Lirianthe*, and *Blumiana* (the first two of *Magnolia*, the last one of the former Asian *Talauma*)
Clade 7	*Dugandiodendron*, *Magnolia* sections *Splendentes* and *Talauma* (the former New World *Talauma*).
Clade 8	*Manglietia*
Clade 9	*Magnolia* sections *Rhytidospermum* and *Oyama*.
Clade 10	*Magnolia fraseri* and *M. pyramidata*.
Clade 11	*Magnolia macrophylla*, *M. ashei*, and *M. dealbata*.

Figure 1. Subfamily Magnolioideae Clade Table adapted from Kim *et al.* (2001a, 2001b).

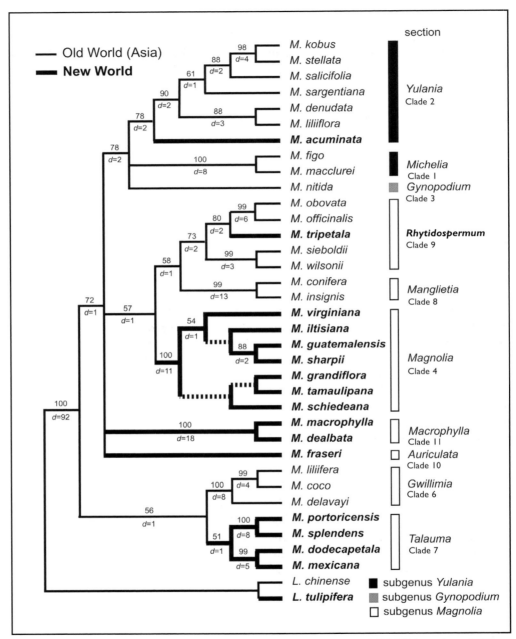

Figure 2. One of 30 most parsimonious trees from Azuma *et al.* (2004) based on 5971 DNA characters. The numbers above the branches are bootstrap percentages and those below the branches are Bremer support. Subgenera and sectional treatments are based on Figlar & Nooteboom (2004).

Additional DNA studies by Hiroshi Azuma and his co-researchers, using different DNA segments, produced phylogenetic trees that were concordant with the topology of Kim's cladogram (Azuma *et al*, 1999, 2001) even though fewer taxa were used. Moreover, Azuma's most recent study (2004) revealed improved phylogenetic resolution especially among the basal 7 clades (*Kmeria*, Clade 5, was not sampled in Azuma's analysis). See Figure 2, opposite.

If this weren't enough, an independent stomatographical study of all known Magnoliaceae lineages (Baranova and Jeffery, 2000) revealed 12 groups based on their stomata morphology. Not surprisingly, the groups closely matched Kim's 11 clades.

Concurrent with all this research, Nooteboom and I continued to re-examine morphology mainly by looking at living plants. We also looked at data from previous works. But Kim's 11 molecular clades became a new "template" for Magnoliaceae. What morphological characters could explain this topology? We found many:

Stamen attachment: Taxa of the Clades 1 and 2 all have stamens that remain attached to the androphore during and after the male phase of the flower. Taxa of the other 9 clades all* produce stamens that detach from the androphore during the male phase (often falling into the concave tepals below). *In *Magnolia sieboldii* and other section *Oyama*, the stamens are at least partially persistent – likely a parallel development in this group. [Since observations of this character almost always need to be made on living flowering plants, I am grateful for help received from others in this effort, especially Sima Yong-Kang. In some cases, meaningful observations could be discerned from photographs of flowers.]

Pollen: A review of pollen data (Praglowski, 1974) revealed that taxa of Clades 1 and 2 have pollen with a diameter less than 50µm. In contrast, taxa of the basal 8 clades produce pollen with diameters greater than 50µm, while pollen diameter for taxa in Clade 3 was immediate in size (39 to 46µm based on *Pachylarnax praecalva*).

Leaf prefoliation (vernation): Taxa in all clades but one, Clade 3, produce new leaves that emerge from the bud in the conduplicate position (folded in half). However, in all taxa of Clade 3, the *Gynopodium / Pachylarnax / Manglietiastrum* clade, the new leaves emerge in the open position. That is, the adaxial sides of the new leaf are pressed against the ensuing bud, instead of pressed against each other (conduplicate) as in all other Magnolioideae taxa. Open prefoliation was first described by Johnstone (1955) in *Magnolia nitida*. However, Dandy never mentioned it in his works or his unpublished notes. Later, Liu (Law, 1979) described open prefoliation in *Manglietiastrum*. There was no data on *Pachylarnax* until Sangtae Kim was able to observe the open leaf in a carefully dissected bud from an old voucher specimen in Nooteboom's lab. This was later confirmed in living plants (Sima *et al.*, 2001).

Proleptic/Sylleptic branching: It was confirmed that all lineages represented in Clades 1 and 2 normally produce branches by prolepsis, while taxa in the 9 remaining clades normally produce branches by syllepsis (except in section *Oyama* where proleptic branching likely developed independently). This character is difficult or impossible to discern from herbarium specimens. [Since prolepsis and persistent stamens are shared by all taxa in the top two clades of the cladogram, they are said to be derived characters, or synapomorphies. Interestingly, the character, prolepsis, is also a synapomorphy in *Rhododendron* and occurs in the top two clades of its phylogenetic tree, as well (Goetsch, *et al.*, 2005).]

Temporal character: Precocious flower production (late-winter, early spring before new leaves appear) occurs in all non-tropical lineages represented in Clades 1 and 2. Flowers occur in late spring (and often beyond) in non-tropical lineages of the basal 8 clades (Clades 4-11). The temporal character was observed to be intermediate in section *Gynopodium* (Clade 3). Obviously, there are difficulties in assessing this character in truly tropical taxa.

Fruit shape & phyllotaxus: Even though carpel dehiscence and concrescence seem to mostly have arisen independently in various lineages, the looser arrangement of carpels into a more/less cylindrical shape versus the more packed arrangement of carpels into a more cone-like shape seems to be taxonomically important. Here again, we find that fruits of taxa in Clades 1 and 2 are usually cylindrical in shape with carpels arranged loosely in low order phyllotactic patterns, while the taxa in the rest of the clades bear fruits more/less cone-like in shape usually in higher order phyllotactic patterns, especially in species with an abundance of carpels (Figlar, 2002b; Holliger, 2003).

Stipule scar on petiole: Free stipules (leaving no scar on the leaf petioles) have long been used to separate *Magnolia* section *Theorhodon* from other *Magnolia* sections. However, by studying petioles on live plants of *M. grandiflora*, *M. tamaulipana* and others of this section, we did consistently find very short stipule scars on the base of the petioles. This provided a morphological basis for

supporting the combination of *Magnolia virginiana* (section *Magnolia*) with section *Theorhodon*. We also found very short stipule scars on petioles of several *Michelia* spp. that "weren't supposed to have them." On the other hand, our observations supported free stipules in section *Gynopodium*. In herbarium specimens these observations would not be possible due to specimen degradation.

These and other morphological findings – some of them new to Magnoliaceae science – provide a strong morphological basis to account for the close relationship among the lineages in Clade 1; *Michelia, Elmerrillia, Aromadendron,* and *Magnolia* sections *Alcimandra,* and *Maingola*; and Clade 2, *Magnolia* subgenus *Yulania* (see Figure 1, page 73). Similarly, the findings reveal a common, subgenus *Magnolia*-like, set of characters that are shared by taxa of the basal 8 clades, Clades 4 through 11. Lastly, these data uncovered the morphological uniqueness – open leaf prefoliation – common to the lineages in Clade 3, *Magnolia* section *Gynopodium, Pachylarnax,* and *Manglietiastrum.* Its morphological distinctiveness is further underscored by the fact that all 9 species represented in Clade 3 are completely glabrous (hairless) plants with free stipules. Thus, we felt strongly that subfamily Magnolioideae of Magnoliaceae should contain just one genus, *Magnolia*, subdivided into three subgenera: *Yulania, Magnolia, and Gynopodium.* To account for remaining morphological variation, we subdivided the three subgenera into sections and subsections (Figlar and Nooteboom, 2004). All 12 sections described are congruent with the 11 DNA clades (since Clade 3 became a subgenus, an additional section was created to accommodate the former *Parchylarnax* and *Manglietiastrum*). See Figure 3, pages 78–79.

DNA studies clearly show that genera *Michelia, Manglietia, Talauma,* and the various splinter genera are all nested within *Magnolia*. Hypothetically, if one were to insist on retaining a genus *Michelia,* or *Manglietia,* the name *Magnolia* would become irrelevant since it would refer to a paraphyletic group (one that no longer contains its common ancestor and *all* its descendants). In such a case, the name *Magnolia campbellii* would then have to become *Yulania campbellii*. Equally imprudent, if we had decided to name the 11 clades as individual genera, we would have introduced needless complexity to a very natural and genetically close subfamily. For example, in DNA sequencing, one is able to estimate genetic divergence between any two taxa in the study matrix by using "% sequence distance" (number of base substitutions divided by number of bases, all multiplied by 100). The average divergence between most sections of genus *Magnolia* (0.63%) is about the same as that between *Michelia* and subgenus *Yulania* (0.61%) based on data from Hiroshi Azuma (unpublished). Moreover, for *Magnolia* section *Rhytidospermum*, Azuma's data reveals slightly less genetic divergence between it and *Manglietia* (0.41%) than between it and *Magnolia* section *Theorhodon* (0.53%). In contrast the divergence between *Liriodendron* and *Magnolia* averaged 2.25%. Thus, the consistently low divergence within Magnolioideae is added justification for the one-genus concept. Therefore, it would be inappropriate to assign generic rank to each of the 11 clades or to any combination of clades, short of all eleven.

Coming full circle, the story that started in 1886 with Ballion, now ends with Ballion in 2004. The system of subfamily Magnolioideae is best described as containing one genus, *Magnolia,* just as Ballion had theorised. I think if Dandy had been able to observe more living plants, instead of dried herbarium specimens, he would have eventually arrived at this classification or something close to it. He seemed to have been on to something in 1927 based on his mentioning, "*Aromadendron* is much further removed from *Talauma* … and shows its closest affinities with such species as *Magnolia gustavii*" [now of subsection *Maingola* of *Magnolia*]. But he never codified that affinity in his classifications. If he had dug further, maybe he could have made the connection between *Aromadendron/Maingola* and *Michelia, Alcimandra* and the others in that clade.

One will undoubtedly notice (Figure 3, see next page) that a *Buergeria* subdivision is not defined in the new classification. This is because DNA results - which showed *M. cylindrica* clustering with *M. denudata,* while *M. zenii* and *M. amoena* clustered with *Buergeria* spp. – suggest that sepaloid tepals cannot be used to key a separate subsection *Buergeria*. This character probably evolved independently throughout the now greater section *Yulania*. Perhaps more research is needed on these diploid species.

Also noticeable is the dropping of the sectional name *Theorhodon* in favor of section *Magnolia*. This was required by nomenclature rules since *M. virginiana* and its section *Magnolia* are the type for the genus.

A complete list of species comprising genus *Magnolia* can be found on the

Genus **Magnolia**

Subgenus **Magnolia**

Branches normally produced by syllepsis (except in subsect. *Oyama*). Leaf vernation (prefoliation) conduplicate. Flowers terminal on long shoots. Introrse anther dehiscence. Gynoecium sessile. Fruit more/less cone shaped with fused carpels until dehiscence, usually longitudinally sometimes circumscissile. Mid-late season flowering in non-tropical spp. (Generally, one cannot easily discern the presence of flower buds until the season in which the flowers are produced). Pollen large, diameter usually> 50µm. Stamens caducous during male phase (except in subsect. *Oyama*). Usually 2 ovules per carpel (except in sect. *Manglietia*).

Section **Magnolia** (ca.16 spp. SE US & Central America)

Leaves evergreen or sometimes deciduous in one sp., *M. virginiana*. Stipules adnate to most of the petiole in one sp., *M. virginiana,* or adnate to the base of the petiole, thus appearing to be free in all other spp. of this section. Stomata group number 5 (see Baranova & Jeffrey, 2000).

Section **Gwillimia** (ca. 16 spp. SE Asia to Malesia) Leaves evergreen. Stipules adnate to the petiole. Stomata group number 9.

Subsection **Gwillimia** (includes former sect. *Lirianthe)*

Stipules adnate to (mostly) the entire length of the petiole. Carpels longitudinally dehiscent. Stylar beaks, in fruit, often flattened.

Subsection **Blumiana**

Stipules adnate to 50% to 100% the length of the petiole. Carpels dehiscing mostly circumscissile.

Section **Talauma**

Leaves evergreen. Long connective appendage (embedded in the gynoecium) except in subsect. *Talauma*. Carpels dehiscing circumscissile except in subsect. *Cubenses*. Stomata group numbers 5, 3, and 2.

Subsection **Talauma** (ca. 31 spp. Cent. & S. America, W. Indies)

Stipules adnate to the petiole. Carpels dehiscing circumscissile. Stomata group number 5.

Subsection **Dugandiodendron** (ca. 14 spp. South America)

Stipules free (or appearing so) from the petiole. Long connective appendage embedded in gynoecium (except in *calophyllum, M. magnifolium* and *M. calimaense*). Carpels dehiscing circumscissile. Stomata group numbers 2 and 3.

Subsection **Cubenses***

(ca, 10 spp. W Indies) [Corrected from subsect. Splendentes.] Stipules free (or appearing so) from the petiole. Long connective appendage embedded in gynoecium. Carpels longitudinally dehiscent. Stomata group number 2.

Section **Manglietia** (ca. 29 spp. China, SE Asia)

Leaves evergreen (except in one sp., *M. decidua).* Early season leaves sometimes arranged in false whorls (flushing). Usually 4 or more ovules per carpel. Stomata group number 8.

Section **Kmeria** (3 spp. China, Indochina, Thailand)

Leaves evergreen. Stipules attached to > 50% of the petiole. Flowers unisexual. Stomata group number 11.

Section **Rhytidospermum**

Leaves deciduous. Branches produced by syllepsis or prolepsis. Stomata group number 7.

Subsection **Rhytidospermum** (ca. 4 spp. temperate E US & E Asia)

Branches produced mostly by syllepsis. Early-season leaves arranged in false whorls (flushing). Stamens caduceus during male phase.

Subsection **Oyama** (4 spp. temperate E & SE Asia)

Branches produced mostly by prolepsis. Leaves arranged 'normally' (no flushing). Stamens mostly persistent during male phase.

Section **Auriculata** (2 spp. temperate SE US)

Leaves deciduous with auriculate bases (glabrous). Early season leaves arranged in false whorls (flushing). Flowers semi-precocious. Tepals without purple spot on base of adaxial surface. Stomata group number 6.

Section **Macrophylla** (3 spp. temperate SE US & Mexico)

Leaves deciduous with cordate to auriculate bases (glaucous to m/l pubescent). Early season leaves only moderately flushed. Tepals with purple spot on base of adaxial surface. Stomata group number 4.

Subgenus **Yulania**

Branches normally produced by prolepsis (less pronounced in tropical spp.) Leaf vernation (prefoliation) conduplicate. Flowers terminal and/or on abbreviated branchlets. Fruit more/less cylindrical in shape (often apocarpus, longitudinally dehiscent, or occasionally with concrescent carpels resulting in a more ellipsoidal shape which is dehiscent circumscissile). Precocious flowering, generally before new leaves appear (Usually, one can discern the presence of flower buds during the summer preceding the year the flowers are produced). Pollen small, diameter usually < 50µm. Stamens persistent during male phase.

Section **Yulania**

Leaves deciduous. Flowers terminal or sometimes on abbreviated branchlets. Latrorse anther dehiscence. Fruits cylindrical, carpels longitudinally dehiscent (& circumscissile in *M. cylindrica*). Usually 2 ovules per carpel. Stomata group number 13.

Subsection **Yulania** (ca. 13 spp. temperate E Asia)

Tepals white, pink, or purple (sometimes outer whorl sepaloid) Pronounced precocious flowering.

Subsection **Tulipastrum** (1 sp. temperate E North America)

Tepals green to yellow (outer whorl sepaloid). Precocious flowering less pronounced (but still occurring before vegetative buds open).

Section **Michelia**

Leaves evergreen. Usually 2 to 6 (to many) ovules per carpel.

Subsection **Michelia** (ca. 50 spp. warm temperate to tropical SE Asia)

Flowers mostly on abbreviated branchlets, rarely terminal on long shoots. Gynoecium stipitate. Latrorse anther dehiscence. Fruits cylindrical, apocarpous or occasionally concrescent/circumscissile. Usually 2 to 6 (to many) ovules per carpel. Stomata group number 12.

Subsection **Elmerrillia** (4 spp. Malesia)

Flowers mostly on abbreviated branchlets, rarely terminal on long shoots. Gynoecium sessile. Introrse anther dehiscence. Fruits cylindrical & dehiscent longitudinally or occasionally thickly concrescent/circumscissile. Usually 2 to 6 ovules per carpel. Stomata group number 12.

Subsection **Maingola**** (ca. 7 spp. warm temperate to tropical SE Asia)

Flowers terminal (on long shoots) or rarely on abbreviated branchlets. Gynoecium variably stipitate. Introrse anther dehiscence. Fruits cylindrical. Usually 2 ovules per carpel. Stomata group numbers 12 and 14.

Subsection **Aromadendron** (5 spp. Malesia)

Flowers terminal (on long shoots) or rarely on abbreviated branchlets. Gynoecium stipate except in *M. ashtonii*. Introrse anther dehiscence. Fruits thickly concrescent, dehiscent circumscissile. Stomata group number 14.

Subgenus **Gynopodium**

Leaves evergreen. Branches normally produced by syllepsis. Leaf vernation (prefoliation) open, not conduplicate. Plants entirely glabrous. Stamens caduceus during male phase. Fruit more/less cone shaped with fused carpels until dehiscing longitudinally. Gynoecium shortly stipitate (sessile in *M. praecalva* and *M. pleiocarpa*). Stipules free.

Section **Gynopodium** (ca. 5 spp. S China & Taiwan, Burma, Vietnam)

Tree androdioecious (bisexual in *M. nitida* var. *nitida* & *M. kachirachirai*). Gynoecium shortly stipitate. Carpels dehiscent longitudinally mostly along dorsal suture. Ovules 2 per carpel (up to 4 in *M. kachirachirai*). Stomata group number 11.

Section **Manglietiastrum** (3 spp. S China & adjacent SE Asia, Malesia)

Flowers bisexual. Gynoecium sessile (but shortly stipitate in *M. sinica*). Carpels dehiscent longitudinally mostly along the ventral suture especially at apex of fruit. Usually 3 to 8 ovules per carpel. Stomata group number 10.

* *Magnolia* subsect. *Cubenses* Imkhanitskaya (1991) predates publication of *Magnolia* subsect. *Splendentes* (Dandy ex A. Vazquez) Figlar & Noot. (2004), thus the correct name is the former.

** *Magnolia* section *Alcimandra* had been previously combined with section *Maingola* (Kim et al 2002).

Figure 3. Classification Key for Magnolioideae
(adapted from Figlar & Nooteboom, 2004

Magnolia Society International website www.magnoliasociety.org. All reduced lineages have been renamed as *Magnolia* except for several of the former *Manglietia* species. New combinations for these are currently being prepared and should be published later in 2006.

As Lord Aberconway alluded to in 1950, "…every classification suffers from certain defects." This one is no exception. As pointed out before, even though there is unarguable support for each of the 11 clades, the evolutionary history of the basal 8 clades (subgenus *Magnolia*) is not yet fully resolved. As the science of molecular systematics continues to press forward, this will undoubtedly be sorted out, resulting in improvements to the classification. However, due to the strength of the DNA and morphological evidence described here, it is unlikely that future changes would involve much more than the fine-tuning of sectional and subsectional ranks within the genus *Magnolia*. No more generic name changes should ever again be necessary. Our beloved Magnolias will always be *Magnolia*.

The author thanks Hans P. Nooteboom for innumerable things, among them reviewing this manuscript. He joins me in acknowledging the noteworthy contributions made by Sangtae Kim in the development of the new classification. Many others are to be recognised as well, including Hiroshi Azuma, Leonard B. Thien, Sima Yong-Kang, and Stephen A. Spongberg. This article is dedicated to the memory of James E. Dandy. I wish he could be here today.

References

ABERCONWAY, C. (1950) Introduction to a lecture from J.E. Dandy, A Survey of the Genus *Magnolia* together with *Manglietia* and *Michelia*. In: *Camellias and Magnolias, Conference Report,* p. 78. Royal Horticultural Society, London.

AZUMA, H., THIEN, L.B & KAWANO, S. (1999) Molecular phylogeny of *Magnolia* (Magnoliaceae) inferred from cpDNA sequences and evolutionary divergence of floral scents. *J. Plant Res.* 112: 291-306.

AZUMA, H., THIEN, L.B & KAWANO, S. (2000) Molecular phylogeny of *Magnolia* based on chloroplast DNA sequence data (*trn*K intron, *psb*A-*trn*H and *atp*B-*rbc*L intergenic spacer regions) and floral scent chemistry. In: Y.H. Liu *et al.* (eds.) *Proceedings Internat. Symp. Fam. Magnoliaceae 1998:* 219-227. Science Press, Beijing, China.

AZUMA, H., GARCÍA-FRANCO, J., RICO-GRAY, V. & THIEN, L.B. (2001) Molecular Phylogeny of the Magnoliaceae: The biogeography of tropical and temperate disjunctions. *Amer. J. Bot.* 88(12): 2275-2285.

AZUMA, H. L., RICO-GRAY, V., GARCÍA-FRANCO, J.G., TOYOTA, M., ASAKAWA, Y. & THIEN, L.B. (2004) *Acta Phytotax. Geobot.* 55(3): 167-180.

BAILLON, H.E. (1866) Mémoire sur famille des Magnoliacées. *Adansonia* 7: 1-16, 65-69.

BARANOVA, M.A. & JEFFERY, C. (2000) Stomatographical features in the systematics of the Magnoliaceae. *Bot. Zhurn.* 85: 35-49.

BENTHAM, G. & HOOKER, J.D. (1862) *Genera Plantarum* 1: 18-19.

BLUME, C.L. (1825) Bijdragen tot de flora van Nederlandsch-Indië. *Lands Drukkerij.*

CHUN, W.Y. (1963) Genus speciesque novae Magnoliacearum Sinensium. *Acta Phytotax. Sinica* 8(4): 281-283.

DANDY, J.E. (1927) The genera of Magnolieae. *Bull. Of Misc. Inform.* No. 7. Kew: 257-264.

DANDY, J.E. (1950) A Survey of the Genus *Magnolia* together with *Manglietia* and *Michelia*. In: *Camellias and Magnolias, Conference Report,* pp. 64-81. Royal Horticultural Society, London.

DANDY, J.E. (1978) A revised survey of the genus *Magnolia* together with *Manglietia* and *Michelia*. In: N.G. Treseder, *Magnolias:* 29-37.

FIGLAR, R.B. (2000) Proleptic branch initiation in *Michelia* and *Magnolia* subgenus *Yulania* provides basis for combinations in subfamily Magnolioideae. In: Y.H. Liu *et al.* (eds.) *Proceedings Internat. Symp. Fam. Magnoliaceae 1998:* 14-25. Science Press, Beijing, China.

FIGLAR, R.B. (2002a) Those amazing *Magnolia* fruits. *Magnolia – J. Mag. Soc.* 37: 7-15.

FIGLAR, R.B. (2002b) Phyllotaxus in *Magnolia* fruits. *Magnolia – J. Mag. Soc.* 37: 26-28.

FIGLAR, R.B. & NOOTEBOOM, H.P. (2004) Notes on Magnoliaceae IV. *Blumea* 49: 87-100.

GOETSCH, L., ECKERT, A.J., & HALL, B.D. (2005) The molecular systematics of *Rhododendron* (Ericaceae): A phylogeny based upon *RPB2* gene sequences. *Sys. Bot.* 30(3): 616-626.

HOLLIGER, P. (ed.) (2003) Errata for ref. 2002a & 2002b. *Magnolia – J. Mag. Soc.* 38. p.24.

HU, H.H. (1940) *Paramichelia,* a new genus of Magnoliaceae. *Sunyatsenia* 4: 142-145.

HU, H.H. & CHENG, W.Y. (1951a) *Parakmeria,* a new genus of Magnoliaceae of southwestern China. *Acta Phytotax. Sinica* 1: 1-2.

HU, H.H. & CHENG, W.Y. (1951b) *Paramanglietia,* a new genus of Magnoliaceae. *Acta Phytotax. Sinica* 1: 255-256.

IMKHANITSKAYA, N.N. (1991) *Novosti Sis. V ssh. Rast.* 28: 60.

JOHNSTONE, G.H. (1955) *Asiatic Magnolias in Cultivation.* Royal Horticultural Society, London.

KENG, H. (1978) The delimitation of genus *Magnolia* (Magnoliaceae). Gard. Bull. Straits Settlem. 31: 127-131.

KIM, S., PARK, C.W. & SUH, Y. (1998) Molecular phylogeny of *Magnolia* and related genera based on its sequences. *Int. Symp. Fam. Magnoliaceae Guangzhou program & abstracts.* Guangzhou, China.

KIM, S., PARK, C.W. & SUH, Y. (2001a) Phylogenetic relationships in Magnoliaceae inferred from *ndhF* sequences. *Amer. J. Bot.* 88: 717-728.

KIM, S., PARK, C.W. & SUH, Y. (2001b) Phylogeny and evolution of the Magnoliaceae implied by sequences of 10 chloroplast DNA regions. *Botany 2001 Abstracts,* pub. by Bot. Soc. of Amer. Aug. 2001: Abstract # 484, p. 121.

KIM, S., NOOTEBOOM, H.P., PARK, C.W. & SUH, Y. (2002) Taxonomic revision of *Magnolia* section *Maingola* (Magnoliaceae). *Blumea* 47: 319-339.

KUMAR, S. & FILIPSKI, A.J. (2001) Molecular Phylogeny Reconstruction. *Encyclopedia of Life Sciences.* Macmillan Publishers Ltd, Nature Pub. Group.

LAW, Y.W. (1979) A new genus of Magnoliaceae from China. *Acta. Phytotax. Sin.* 11: 72-74.

LAW, Y.W. (1984) A preliminary study on the taxonomy of the family Magnoliaceae. *Acta. Phytotax. Sin.* 22: 80-109.

LAW, Y.W. (1996) Magnoliaceae. In: *Flora Reipublicae Popularis Sinicae,* vol.30(1), 82-269.

NOOTEBOOM, H.P. (1985) Notes on Magnoliaceae. *Blumea* 31: 65-121.

PRAGLOWSKI, J. (1974) *Magnoliaceae Juss. World Pollen and Spore Flora* 3: 1-48.

PRANTL, K.A.E. (1888) In: A. Engler & K. Prantl (eds), *Die Natürlichen Pflanzenfamilien* 3, 2.

QIU, Y.L. (1993) Molecular divergence between Asian and North American species of *Magnolia* section *Rytidospermum* (Magnoliaceae). Ph.D. dissertation, University of North Carolina. Chapel Hill, North Carolina, USA.

QIU, Y.L., CHASE, M.W. & PARKS, C.R. (1995a) A chloroplast DNA phylogenetic study of the eastern Asia – eastern North America disjunct section *Rytidospermum* of *Magnolia* (Magnoliaceae). *Amer. J. Bot.* 82: 1582-1588.

QIU, Y.L., CHASE, M.W. & PARKS, C.R. (1995b) Molecular divergence in the eastern Asia – eastern North America disjunct section *Rytidospermum* of *Magnolia* (Magnoliaceae). *Amer. J. Bot.* 82: 1589-1598.

SIMA, Y.K., WANG, J., CAO, L.M., WANG, B.Y., & WANG, Y.U. (2001) Prefoliation Features of the Magnoliaceae and their Systematic Significance. *Jour. of Yunnan Univ.* 23: 71-78.

SPONGBERG, S.A. (1998) Magnoliaceae hardy in cooler temperate regions. In: Hunt, D. (ed) Magnolias and their allies, *Proceedings of an Internat. Symp.*: 81-144.

UEDA, K., YAMASHITA, J. & TAMURA. M.N. (2000) Molecular phylogeny of the Magnoliaceae. In: Y.H. Liu *et al.* (eds) *Proceedings Internat. Symp. Fam. Magnoliaceae 1998*: 205-209. Science Press, Beijing, China.

Dick Figlar is a former President of the Magnolia Society and, in retirement, cultivates an outstanding magnolia collection at his garden in South Carolina

BOOK REVIEW

The International Rhododendron Register and Checklist Second Edition

Full marks to Dr Alan C. Leslie and his team in producing this edition of the International Rhododendron Register which updates and considerably improves on the First Edition which was published in 1958 – a gap of 47 years! It had become increasingly difficult to track down details of new Rhododendron hybrids registered over that period because it meant consulting no less than 40 supplementary lists.

It took a total of 21 years to revise and update all the relevant data in accordance with the latest international rules of nomenclature and to take into account the Edinburgh revision of the genus rhododendron

At the same time it has been made user-friendly by the inclusion of a broad concept of synonyms which are in common use and which lead to the correct registered name for that particular cultivar or group. The term 'grex' has been eliminated in favour of the term 'Group', since the term grex is now restricted for the use of orchids alone.

Hybrids registered in the 19th century were allowed to be given Latin names. At that time azaleas were regarded as being a separate genus from rhododendrons. The decision that they should be classified under the genus *Rhododendron* (subsequently confirmed to be correct by DNA research) involved some changes in these Latin names for the odd reason that the name azalea is feminine whereas rhododendron is neuter. Thus, for example, the Azaleas *R. viscosa, R.* 'Delicatissima' and *R.* 'Exquisita' have been neutered and their correct spellings are now *R. viscosum, R.* 'Delicatissimum' and *R.* 'Exquisitum', as listed in the *RHS Plant Finder*. Some Nursery lists have not fully reflected this change in nomenclature and should act now to avoid confusion.

The very clear and concise introduction to the Register sets out the rules and meanings by which the 28,000 entries are described. A useful glossary follows. After the main listings there is a 51-page index of the names and addresses of individuals, nurseries and estates mentioned in the Register. Finally, there is a select bibliography of the major source books on cultivar and group names which are cited in the Register. The two volumes cover a total of 1,544 pages.

When confronted with the vast total of 28,000 cultivars, groups and synonyms, one wonders what proportion of this number relates to earlier varieties which never became widely distributed after registration or which were superseded by similar but improved later varieties. In this context it might be useful to consider in what proportion the total number breaks down into the main components. A rough guesstimate might be:

Azaleas	9,000
Rhodendendrons	19,000
Total	**28,000**

To see how this compares with the estimated number of entries in some of the main reference books, see the table on the next page.

Table of Estimated Numbers of Rhododendron and Azalea Hybrids in some of the Main Reference Books

Date	Reference Book	Azaleas	Rhodos	Total Hybrids
1961	Leach's *Rhododendrons of the World*	–	2750	2750
1987	Galle's *Azaleas*	6000	–	6000
1988	Cox's *Encyclopedia of Rhododendron Hybrids*	–	2650	2650
1992	Salley & Greer's *Rhododendron Hybrids* 2nd Edn	–	5000	5000
1992	Van Gelderen & Van Hoey Smith's *Rhododendrons*	–	1050	1050
1996	Greer's *Guidebook to Available Rhododendrons* 3rd Edn	–	2500	2500
1997	*Cumulative Index of RHS Rhododendron Yearbooks*	650	1950	2600
2003–4	*RHS Plant Finder*	500	2000	2500

Notes

1. There are now later editions of some of these books.
2. The above figures were arrived at in various ways and may not be fully accurate.
3. The Van Gelderen book is published as *Rhododendron Portraits* in the USA. With a colour plate for every entry it is top of the list in that respect.
4. Cox's Encyclopedia is most comprehensive as to data and knowledgeable advice on the merits and demerits of each variety. Their proposed new edition is eagerly awaited.

In considering these figures it is important to bear in mind the vast difference between the favoured maritime climates of the Atlantic coast of the British Isles, the Pacific coastal region of Northwest USA and New Zealand as compared with the much more rigorous climates of the large Continental masses, with their need for Hardy Hybrids, and the fact that some countries have developed their own ranges of hybrids to suit their local conditions e.g. Belgium, Germany, Holland and New Zealand and that many of these varieties are supplementary to those listed in the reference books in the table above.

Finally, when trying to identify hybrids in old gardens, it is useful to have a checklist of details of varieties that are no longer available in commerce. When one finds an abundance of *R. luteum* and little or no sign of yellow rhododendron hybrids it can be deduced that the main plantings took place before the 1920s when many yellow species were introduced and therefore became available to produce yellow hybrids. A later cut-off point comes with the advent of micropropagation, lessening the practice of grafting hybrids onto *R. ponticum* rootstock with its subsequent problem of reversion to the ponticum. These two events can be of great assistance in ruling out the many hybrids introduced at a later date. Somehow it is reassuring to know that the name and description of the plant in question lies somewhere within the pages of the two volumes of the Register. Obviously all the other reference books have to omit most of the older and obscure varieties which have been relegated to history.

Now that all the relevant data has been transformed from index cards to electronic format, it is to be hoped that it will be possible to publish the Third Edition of this fully extensive work of reference within the next 20 years, thus avoiding the need to pursue many supplementary lists to find details of the latest registered hybrids. The rather thin cardboard covers of the two volumes seem to suggest that a shorter time span is envisaged.

It is quite a common practice for people to give rhododendrons to friends to mark a happy occasion or to want to plant one in memory of someone dear to them. It is much appreciated if the plant name is appropriate. Good examples are 'Birthday Girl', 'Silver Wedding', 'Golden Wedding', 'George's Delight', 'Elizabeth' and 'Christmas Cheer'. There are many other candidates. The Register is an excellent source of ideas for this purpose but, of course, availability has to be checked to obtain a suitable plant, readily.

Hybridists might be described appropriately as "Busy Bees" to have reached a total of nearly 28,000 registrations over a period of (say) 140 years. The applications for new registrations must be arriving at RHS Wisley at the rate of around 200 per year, presenting quite a task in checking all the details and maintaining all the records in apple pie order.

The Register might be likened to the English Dictionary in the sense that you cannot just sit down and read it from cover to cover; it provides vital, trustworthy information when you need to consult it for a particular entry.

So let us give a warm welcome to this new edition of the Register.

Nigel Wright is the proprietor of Nigel Wright Rhododendrons Ltd at the Old Glebe, Eggesford, Devon. A specialist grower of Rhododendron hybrids. He is also a former chairman of the Southwest Branch of the Group

Obituary

Os Blumhardt – Plant Breeder and Friend
I would like to pay tribute to one of the unsung heroes of horticulture and gardening in New Zealand who died recently. You may not have known him, but it is likely you will have at least one of the plants he bred in your garden. Os was one of a breed of passionate and knowledgeable plantspeople and his breeding covered a wide range of different genera. Some of the resulting plants have become standard lines in production in New Zealand. In magnolias, 'Star Wars' is his best-known cultivar. It is a large-growing, large-flowered pink. In michelias, Os was responsible for the main *M. foggii* hybrids available today – notably 'Mixed Up Miss' and 'Bubbles', valued as smaller growing evergreen trees with white flowers in winter. Among the camellias, he gave us such standards as the slow-growing 'Night Rider', the ubiquitous 'Gay Baby' and the delightful 'Fairy Wand'. The exquisite 'Tiny Star' was a Blumhardt product and he also created the enormous 'Red Crystal'. From the sasanqua group, he gave us the gorgeous 'Sugar Dream'. Along with his old friend Felix Jury, Os pursued a love affair with vireya rhododendrons and few collections in New Zealand would be without 'Saxon Blush' and 'Jiminy Cricket'. Add to those the much sought-after showy 'Rio Rita', the pink and white 'Kisses' among many others, and you start to see what a major contribution Os made to gardens with his work in this subgenus. He also contributed a number of species he collected in the wild. Os also loved the classic full-trussed rhododendrons and was a long-time supporter of Pukeiti. While none of his hybrids in this area have become widely available, he was constantly seeking plants that would perform well in the warmer climate of his Whangarei home.

He did his apprenticeship in Taranaki at Duncan and Davies in the 1950s when that company was a major force as a leader in horticulture both in New Zealand and overseas. Duncan and Davies were responsible for training most of the significant people in New Zealand horticulture at that time. It was then that Os became friends with Mark Jury's parents, Felix and Mimosa, and he followed many similar paths to Felix in plant breeding. That friendship crossed to the next generation and Os would turn up to stay with us every few years.

A quiet, unassuming man, his depth of plant knowledge was profound, as was his generosity with plants generally and his own hybrids in particular. We have a clutch of vireyas from his last visit, which we are assessing in our conditions. The naming of plants is a difficult exercise but Os seemed to have a good way of putting catchy and memorable names on many of his cultivars. We have a very early flowering maddenii rhododendron in the nursery, which he called 'Scented Rebel'. We have never produced it commercially and may never do so, but the name still takes my fancy. Os made various forays collecting plants in Asian destinations where the altitude means growing conditions similar to those we have in parts of New Zealand. His last such trip a few years ago was to the highlands of Vietnam, and we grow a very nice *Gordonia* species he brought back from that trip. I guess most of us hope to leave the world a slightly better place for our having been here.

Os certainly achieved that in his quiet way. He died suddenly and somewhat prematurely, but for a deeply religious man to be taken from this world while at worship in his church seems an oddly appropriate way to go.

Abbie Jury

GROUP TOUR TO DEVON AND CORNWALL

OVERVIEW

The Tour began on Sunday evening in Plymouth. The Quality Hotel, high on Plymouth Hoe, was chosen for its superb views over Plymouth Sound.

The 22 tour participants were joined, for certain days and gardens, by a number of Executive Committee and Southwest Branch members; keeping track of everyone and their arrangements became taxing. A most helpful local coach driver conveyed us boldly but carefully along West Country lanes, and everyone enjoyed staying at the Arundell Arms, Lifton, for the Tour's middle section.

The gardens visited were chosen for the important part they have played in the rhododendron story, previously well-known by name but not visited by the Group for many years. Their creators, in many cases had, like the major garden owners, supported the famous plant hunters and raised rhododendrons from wild-collected seed, exchanged plants and hybridised.

Mr Peter Clough, who has spent his life as head gardener and rhododendron expert at Inverewe and elsewhere, spoke to us about the many Cornish gardening families, which have contributed to the rhododendron scene.

Dr John Marston, aided by Mr Martyn Rix, gave a talk one evening on their recent plant hunting trip to Sichuan.

It was intended that the Tour members should learn a little, as well as enjoy the Tour, and to that end a full pack of notes about every garden was included in their file wallet, as well as maps showing their situation.

Mr Peter - Hoblyn had given me a very full description of Lamellen, which was photocopied for everyone.

The individual reports omit gardens that were reported on in recent editions of the Yearbook.

Joey Warren

Colebrook House (18 April 2005)

We were all delighted that Kenwyn Clapp invited us to see his garden. It was our first garden, and we fitted it into our busy schedule at 9 o'clock on Monday morning. Margaret and John Bodenham (our guests that night for dinner and Peter Clough's talk) greeted us at the entrance.

Kenwyn welcomed us, halfway up the drive, to talk about his 3 acre garden, around which Plympton houses have been built over the years. He and Betty lived there for 50 years. He led the way onto the lawn, where a huge chestnut tree that had dominated the area and almost killed the grass, had been cleverly pruned and grass resown to give a large lawn again. The big rhododendrons and camellias bordering the drive are continued round the lawn. A rare *R. hemsleyanum* is, he believes, the first to have flowered in England.

We were free to wander around and enjoy his garden, but should not miss the greenhouse, where John Bodenham had placed some of his pots of flowering vireya rhododendrons, with their spectacularly bright colours and scents.

Kenwyn pointed to a small *Cornus* 'Kenwyn Clapp'. This is grown from a seedling he had found, self-sown, beneath other *Cornus* species; he had taken it to a nursery to grow on, and, if any good, to propagate from. They had done so, and registered it in Kenwyn's name.

Kenwyn has a story about all his plants – but our hour's enjoyment of this peaceful garden was up. In thanking Kenwyn, we gave him a Magnolia 'Heaven Scent'.

Joey Warren

Higher Knowle (18 April 2005)

A very well planted garden of some 3 acres, in an ideal situation for the three genera as well as allied plants such as kalmias, embothriums and the like; there is a high rainfall backed by a water supply off Dartmoor, a well-drained hillside with a low ph. The house was built in 1914 and the garden has been developed by successive owners since then; the present owners, Rosemary and David Quicke, adding substantially.

As you approach the house the ground to the left rises and between the planting of trees and shrubs can be seen stretches of meadow planted with bluebells, primula and wood anemones. Magnolias feature prominently in the recent planting and I noted 'Spectrum', 'Elizabeth', 'Galaxy', 'Gold Star', 'Athene' and 'Apollo'. Among the older plants 'Diva' was featured although the collection of magnolias was for the most part recent.

Camellias featured included *C. oleifera*, 'Konronkoku', and 'Margaret Davis'. This was the first time I had seen this lovely flower and was, later in the week, able to buy a plant. Not surprisingly, many of the well established plants we saw also featured in other gardens, being distributed from Cornish sources; plants such as *Rhododendron* 'Sir Charles Lemon', *R.* 'Countess of Waddington', *Camellia* 'Cornish Snow' and the like. It was interesting to see trees with the tops taken out to grow as shrubs.

The collection was very well labelled with aluminium tags with the names painted in black enamel. They seem to last for ever!

The visit concluded with a presentation of a rhododendron to our host whose cakes were much appreciated.

John Harsant

Lukesland (18 April 2005)

Mrs Rosemary Howell and her son, John, and his wife Lorna, welcomed us with coffee and biscuits. The garden, high on the edge of Dartmoor (200m above sea level with a rainfall of 60–65in), is in and around the valley of a rushing Dartmoor stream, dammed to make the ponds and enhance the waterfalls, with a small gorge below the house, surprisingly lush, planted with huge banks of azaleas and rhododendrons. Many have come from Exbury. For a recent full description of the garden see *Rhododendrons with Camellias and Magnolias 2002,* page 64.

Joey Warren

Mount Edgecumbe (19 April 2005)

The morning sun shone brilliantly as we breakfasted looking out over Plymouth Sound. It was from this same harbour that the writer's great grandfather and bride sailed for Australia in 1838 in the 'Royal George'.

A short passenger ferry took us across the Tamar River into Cornwall at Cremyll where we were greeted by the park manager Mr Ian Berry and head gardener Mr Lee Stenning. We were given a brief history of the park, which was acquired jointly by the Cornwall County and Plymouth City Council, after the Second World War. As our interest was mainly in the National Camellia Collection we were taken up to a higher part of this area in four-wheel-drive vehicles where Lee Stenning then gave us a brief history of the collection.

The concept of a National Camellia Collection came from the late doyen of the camellia world, David Trehane. In 1976 the members of the International Camellia Society gave 100 cultivars; these were planted in the formal gardens but did not flourish because of soil conditions. In the following year another 100 cultivars were dug up from David Trehane's garden and replanted in the Higher Amphitheatre where most of the collection is housed today. Here they do flourish, with adequate rainfall, good drainage and dappled shade from old deciduous trees. Since the original plantings, the collection has been steadily increased by plants and cuttings received from the RHS garden at Wisley, the Crown Estate at Windsor Great Park and the National Trust. Today there are over 1,000 cultivars and species, generally at least two of each.

The main estate road leads up from Cremyll to Mount Edgcumbe House. Early plantings were on the top and bottom of the banks leading off from this, making access difficult. Some of these camellias are now trees, with steps leading up to particular areas. This is still not really 'user friendly' so small plants are placed beside the pathways.

Cultivars are placed mostly in groups with sections for old English cultivars, and those from the USA, Australia and New Zealand, Europe and the Orient. In addition there are collections of the different forms of camellia blooms. Also housed is the collection of cultivars from the late English hybridiser, Gillian Carlyon.

The newer plantings are all being kept as compact bushes by pruning assisted by the invading deer! This is to make the blooms of all new plantings easily accessible to viewers and there are 250,000 of these per year. The camellias were past their best but there were still plenty for us to admire.

Lee Stenning, who has to care for the other gardens in the park which are also a great credit to him, has the camellia collection mapped and cross referenced on his computer. In 2003 The International Camellia Society made the award of 'Camellia Garden of Excellence' to Mount Edgcumbe.

Ross Hayter

Antony House and Woodland Garden (19 April 2005)

Antony House overlooks the Lynher River and was owned by the Carew Pole family for almost 600 years. The family still occupy part of the house but it was gifted to the National Trust just after the Second World War. Repton advised on the landscaping of the grounds around the house in 1792. These include a formal courtyard, terraces and water features.

We were warmly welcomed by Valerie Anderson, the head gardener, and had time to look around the formal garden with its stately yew hedges and well-kept lawns before lunch. The summer gardens within the tall yew hedges were looking very colourful. These were first planted in 1984 and designed by Lady Mary Carew Pole. They contain many roses, clematis and peonies as well as many spring bulbs and shrubs.

After lunch we were taken through the magnolias. *M. denudata* are underplanted with primroses and scillas to provide a wonderful show of white flowers. We continued through a recent planting of *Cornus controversa* to the woodland garden.

This 100-acre woodland garden, bordering the River Lynher is now owned by the Carew Pole Garden Trust and has the National Collection of *Camellia japonica* as well as an outstanding collection of magnolias, rhododendrons and azaleas.

In Higher West Down Wood many magnolias were planted after the Second World War, including *M. campbellii* 'Charles Raffill' and *M. dawsoniana,* which are now over 60ft high. There are also large specimens of *Magnolia campbellii* subsp. *mollicomata* 'Lanarth' and *Magnolia sprengeri* var. *diva, Rhododendron sutchuenense* and groups of *R.* 'Loderi'. Sir John Carew Pole produced very many hybrid rhododendrons that are planted here.

The collection of camellias must be one of the best in the South West and despite the rain were looking very colourful; the bluebells, primroses and other wild flowers carpeted the ground beneath them. Camellias flower here from late winter to June, including fine specimens of 'Jupiter', 'Grand Slam', 'White Nun' to name but a few. There is also a fine collection of white-stemmed birches and an upright form of the tulip tree (*Lirodendron tulipifera* 'Fastigiatum'). Many new magnolias have been planted including some of the new yellow varieties.

We followed the riverside path providing good views of Ince Castle and back to Antony House.

At the Saltpans, which were shaped to collect the salt left by the receding tide there are banks of camellias and rhododendrons including *R. griffithianum* and *R. arboreum.*

Returning to the riverside path we climbed up to Jupiter Point, an outcrop of granite dominated by the standing stone erected in the memory of John and Cynthia Carew Pole, with the inscription 'And still a garden by the water blows'.

At The Crossroads there were many more magnolias including *M. obovata, M. × wieseneri, M. × soulangeana* 'Rustica Rubra' and groups of *Acer palmatum* for autumn colour. *Acer palmatum* 'Senkaki', with its coral bark, contrasted with the underplanting of daffodils

Pat Bucknell

Lancarffe (20 April 2005)

A gem of a garden that is approached down a drive of 20ft-tall *Acer palmatum* and a fine camellia hedge. The lovely Cornish granite house nestles into the hillside.

Richard Gilbert and his wife have lived there since 1956 and have introduced a wonderful collection of plants in the Woodland garden above the house, all well labelled.

Notable among the enormous Turkey oaks (*Quercus cerris*) were *Rhododendron ×* 'Shilsonii' and *R. arboreum* subsp. *cinnamomeum* with a *R. macabeanum* seedling overlooking the tennis court.

Camellia 'Cheryll Lynn and *Rhododendron niveum* were in full bloom near a beautiful walled lily pond with *R.* 'Boddaertianum' growing up one side and *C.* 'St Ewe' cascading down the other. A little haven.

Among other rarities were *R.* × *paradoxum* and *R. spiciferum, R. hyperythrum* and *R. selense* subsp. *dasycladum*. A wonderful collection, beautifully planted in a true garden setting, all in 4.5 acres.

The Group presented Richard Gilbert with a *Rhododendron vernicosum* aff. 'AC 4106' in grateful appreciation of our visit

Michael Jurgens

Lamellen (20 April 2005)

Major Walter Magor encouraged our developing interest in rhododendrons from the 1970s so it was a special delight to visit the Magor garden, Lamellen.

Walter's father, E.J.P. Magor, who spent much of his youth with his aunt at Chyverton, gardened at Lamellen from 1901 –1941 and much of his planting is still in evidence. The garden was neglected for the next 20 years until Walter's return from India and Kenya. His wife Daphne managed the tremendous job of returning the laurel and bamboo-filled garden to some order.

In 1974 their elder daughter Felicity and her husband Jeremy moved into the house and with Walter began to propagate, replace and replant. They replaced shelter belts, reconstructed the stream and repaired the ponds. They planted 200 species and hybrid magnolias, 150 species and many hybrid rhododendrons, camellias, maples, dogwoods, sorbus, cherries, etc to supplement the existing planting. The stream runs through a steep valley and Felicity

mentioned that her father would climb up with a spade and bucket to garden, but Jeremy, with a small bulldozer, has made paths along the sides, which makes for much easier gardening and walking to view the plants.

From here we saw a wonderful *Rhododendron basilicum* overhanging a path with *Magnolia* 'Lamellen Surprise' carrying about 30 large pink flowers nearby. An E.J.P.-planted *R. leptothrium* with new pink growth (renamed by Peter Cox from *R. davidsonianum*), *R. ponticum florepleno* with very small, dark green leaves, *R. hodgsonii, R. arizelum, R. arboreum* 'Goatfell' (a red arboreum from Leonardslee), a very fine *R. fulvum* (deep pink in the bud, light rosy pink flowers, striped darker pink along the back of the petals), and the rare *R. hormophorum,* which was soon to flower and stood 20ft tall. I query this name, now sunk into *R. yunnanense,* because this plant looked completely evergreen but is usually deciduous.

We saw many good rhododendron hybrids like 'Dame Nellie Melba', 'Red Admiral', 'Lamellen', 'Tretawn' 'Damaris' and *R. macabeanum* × *grande* hybrids made by Walter's younger daughter Ann while studying at Kew. There is a good selection of Keith-Rushforth-collected pines and oaks. Of the magnolias, several repeated, we saw 'Butterflies', 'Gold Crown', 'Yellow Fever', 'Koban Dori', 'Gold Star', 'Elizabeth', 'Pegasus', and *M. dawsoniana, M. sprengeri* var. *diva, M.* × *veitchii, M. campbellii* 'Strybing White', two specimens of *M. campbellii* and a beautiful pure white *M. campbellii* Alba Group aquired from Bodnant. Felicity told us the *Cornus capitata* was unhappy in its initial planting space, so was moved at 15ft-high in a digger bucket; it has since doubled in size and is thriving. From here there is a wonderful view down and across the valley. There was so much to see and no space to write it all! This was a very special and happy visit.

Iris Wright

Tremeer (20 April 2005)

In the afternoon we travelled to North Cornwall to visit Tremeer, now the home of Lord (Eddie) and Lady (Vanessa) George, but at one time the garden of Major General Eric Harrison. We last visited in 1998 when it was in the possession of the Haslam-Hopwood family. General Harrison retired here after a distinguished career in the army and immediately fell under the influence of his neighbour at Lamellen. Major Walter Magor, began to plant rhododendrons and camellias. In 1961 he married Roza the widow of J.B. Stevenson whose collection of species is now in the Valley Gardens at Windsor. She brought many Tower Court plants with her, many of which are to be seen here today, including some Kurume azaleas not part of Wilson's famous 'Fifty'.

It is, of course, 25 years since General Harrison retired for the second time, but the garden is now in good hands and all his notebooks, with details of his planting and hybridisation are treasured by the present owners. Lady George warmly welcomed us and we spent a very pleasant and instructive time exploring to see what the Georges have done to recreate General and Mrs Harrison's garden. His so-called "blue" cultivars, originating from Caerhays's *Rhododendron* 'Blue Tit' grex ('St Tudy' (*augustinii* × *impeditum*), 'St Breward' (*augustinii* × *impeditum*) and 'St Merryn ('St Tudy' ×

impeditum), some with a white eye and some with a green eye, are well known. But there are many other interesting plants that we noted, such as Barclay Fox's 'Barclayi' (*arboreum* × *griffithianum*) × (*thomsonii* × 'Glory of Penjerrick'), *R. tsariense* 'Yum Yum' form (said to have originated in this garden), Lord Aberconway's 'Matador' (*griersonianum* × *strigillosum*) (a very good dark red with black anthers from Tower Court), a *R. morii* cross with a pinkish flower, a good *R. roxieanum,* another which some thought was R. 'Conroy' (*cinnabarinum* var. *roylei* × *concatenans*), and a *R. concatenans* × *lutescens* (perhaps unregistered) named 'Annia'.

The garden is the home of many other Cornish hybrids, more than a few on the borderline of being tender. We were able to present Lady George with *R. oligocarpum* brought back from a recent expedition to Yunnan and not hitherto in general cultivation in this country.

Cynthia Postan

Endsleigh (21 April 2005)

The house, at Milton Abbot near Tavistock, was built in 1810 to Sir Jeffry Wyatville's design as a fishing lodge and summer retreat for the Dukes of Bedford and their families. In 1814 Humphrey Repton was asked to landscape the garden. He visited the site a couple of times and left very detailed instructions in one of his famous Red Books.

The long drive to the house was lined on either side by very big old pink rhododendrons (probably 'Endsleigh Pink'). Many had been cut back almost to ground level and were re-growing. The parentage and age is unknown. The property is now owned by Mrs Olga Polizzi. We were welcomed by her daughter, Alexandra, who is converting the house into a luxury hotel. We were shown around by an enthusiastic assistant gardener, Simon Wood, who is very knowledgeable about the plants in and the history of the property.

The garden to the east of the garden is terraced down to the River Tamar. We walked along the top path to the woodland area. This path has large old Irish yews (*Taxus baccata*) planted along it. These have also been cut back severely and are growing again. On the lower side of the path more yews are being planted to form a low hedge to screen garden visitors from the hotel guests. The yews are underplanted with white daffodils making a good contrast with the dark green of the trees.

In the woodland we saw very tall old Douglas Firs (*Pseudotsuga menziesii*) but even though they were two hundred feet high they were not considered 'Champion Trees' as there are taller ones in Scotland. We also noted a large Monkey Puzzle Tree (*Araucaria araucana*). It is thought many of the specimen trees were planted in the 1800s. Old hardy rhododendrons such as R. 'Sappho', azaleas and maples were also in the landscaping.

We returned to the house along a lower path where roses are rambling over an arbour. Roses do well here From here we went to the west of the house to a quite different area. The walk follows a deep valley formed by a tributary of the River Tamar. At the start of the walk we passed a large rockery which is being restored. We passed an old derelict power generating building as we continued up the valley. The stream has been diverted into several leats. These artificial waterways were constructed to take the water along the higher slopes of the valley to create waterfalls and cascades. The sides of the valley have become over grown with *Gunnera manicata* and will have to be thinned. New plantings have been under-taken here as well as elsewhere.

There are about fourteen trees listed as Champion Trees on the estate. Of paricular interest to the late Alan Mitchell, the intrepid tree measurer, were *Fagus sylvatica* 'Pendula', *Cryptomeria japonica* 'Lobbii', *Sequoiadendron giganteum* and many others.

Jane Hayter

Penheale Manor (21 April 2005)

A long, tree-lined drive, which was dappled with primroses and bluebells, led to the Manor House, where we were met by owner Fiona Colville and her head gardener Richard Oldaker, who led the tour.

We gained entrance to the garden by passing a 16th century stable block and walking through the arched gatehouse, The inner walls of this were clothed with climbing plants viz: *Dendromecon rigida*, *Rosa banksia* 'Lutea', *Teucrium* and *Clematis armandii*. Two beds of *Rhododendron forrestii* 'Repens' had been hard pruned to a height of 60cm to 'start again' at ground level.

A box parterre garden had been planted after having received suggested plans and advice from Gertrude Jekyll.

The varied nature of this garden became apparent as we moved through a door to a large pond area surrounded by camellias in flower and then into a garden sub-divided into other sections by 2m-high hedges of yew. It takes Richard and his team of three gardeners six weeks to produce over one tonne of yew clippings, which are taken to be used in the commercial production of cancer treatment drugs.

Camomile lawns and rock gardens containing alpines completed our tour of the formal part of the gardens which was kept in pristine order.

We now progressed to what is the first love of the group members, the woodland garden. We stood on an elevated path overlooking a leat planted with primulas of varying sorts to woodland with snakehead fritillaries underlying a collection of acers. The path led to a 60m-long canal lined with *Rhododendron* 'Cornish Cross' and then into The Dell where rhododendrons are the main feature. Here are extensive plantings that have been carried out since the1960s. A group of *R. cinnabarinum* hybrids looked very good with an outstanding *R.* 'Trewithen Orange'. *R.* 'Rennie Moffat', a *R. valentinianum* × *pachypodum* hybrid that is hardy down to –6°C looked superb, achieving a height of 2m in ten years. Rennie had been head gardener at Penheale for 35 years and the plant was named in his honour. *R.* 'Norman Colville' and *R.* 'Diana Colville' are also named after the previous owners of Penheale.

The star of the whole show, however, was *R.* 'Penheale Blue', a *R. concinnum* × *russatum* hybrid. There are two forms of this – one flowers slightly later than the other – but otherwise they are indistinguishable. It shares a most magnificent deep blue colour in the heart of this rarely visited garden.

Ralph Milward

Werrington (21 April 2005)

How often does a lovely plant found in a garden turn out to have originated at Werrington? I know the finest *Rhododendron lacteum* I have seen did, so it was with eager anticipation that I, and all our party, entered the estate. We were welcomed by Mr and Mrs Michael Williams, and driven the three quarters of a mile to the rhododendron collection in the Terrace Gardens, where, after a short introductory talk, we were let loose in paradise.

The collection contains species grown at Werrington from seed collected by the great plant hunters together with a few later plantings of species and rhododendron hybrids. Much of the planting was done over 80 years ago, and it was sobering to realise that some of the large rhododendrons we walked under could be self sown hybrids from Forrest's and Wilson's species, and that careful work would be needed to sort these out from the original introductions. Inevitably there was far too little time to see everything in the Terrace gardens, so only a fraction of the gems found can be mentioned here.

The one most prominent in my mind is a propagule from a Hooker introduction of *Rhododendron ciliatum,* not just a form with an aristocratic pedigree but one strongly fragrant as well. Close to this is the finest clone of *R. anthosphaerum* I have seen. This had deep rose red corollas in a well rounded truss, close to Eritimum Group.

R. floribundum W4266 is a large upright tree in full flower – full trusses of a clear smoky blue with striking almost black markings. Much rarer is *R. laxiflorum* var. *hardingii* (now a subsp. of *R. annae*) with an excellent full truss of white flowers and the characteristic rough leaf margins – a delight to see this in flower. Near this is what appeared to be *R. lukiangense* but with much more rounded and fuller pink trusses – almost up to the standard of *R. arboreum.*

There was a small tree of *R. pachytrichum* with a compact truss of deep rose, almost red, flowers.

Closer to the entrance is a large area containing plants from subsection neriiflora, including what appeared to be a hedge of mainly *R. neriiflorum* nearly 5m tall. Around this was a bewildering array of species and seedlings from the old sanguineum subseries, with *R. haemaleum* and *R. floccigerum* the outstanding taxa.

An area planted with species from subsection taliensia included *R. alutaceum* in flower, and a superb bush of *R. vellereum* about 3m high with at least 500 flowers.

Notable among the triflora is a number of tall bushes of *R. rubiginosum* Desquamatum Group with widely open flowers close the colour of the best *R. augustinii* clones. There was a shrub of *R. fulvoides* about 10m high, covered in flower at the time of our visit.

A number of interesting magnolias are scattered through the area, but all but a large *Magnolia × veitchii* were over. However it was a pleasure to pay tribute to the original tree of *M. mollicomata* 'Werrington' F25655. Fallen, but regenerating strongly, it will survive for some time yet.

Many of us had to be prised away for refreshments, but we just had time to explore the new plantings around the house, noting a fine specimen of *Magnolia* 'Elizabeth'. The rhododendrons at Werrington are a forcible reminder that George Forrest, with his skilful Chinese helpers, spent so long in the wild that they were able to choose the best forms of each species: we were very grateful to have the chance of appreciating their discernment nearly a century later.

Mike Robinson

Marwood Hill (22 April 2005)

This garden has been lovingly tended and developed throughout its existence. Planting on rough pastureland was begun by Dr Jimmy Smart, an active and much-respected RHS member, in the 1960s, and from 1972 until his death in 2002 he and head gardener Malcolm Pharoah built up one of the largest collections of camellias (600–700 different varieties, including some bred at Marwood Hill) and magnolias (80–100 species and hybrids) in Britain, together with a smaller range of rhododendrons. On arrival at Marwood Hill we were welcomed by Malcolm Pharoah, bearing a splendid bloom of *Magnolia* 'Betty Jessel' – deep rose purple veined white, some 22cm across. We had been hoping to see the similar-sized 'Marwood Spring', a speciality of the garden, derived from a seedling of *M. sprengeri* var. *diva* from Caerhays, but only three ageing flowers remained on the tree – which, we were told, had carried some 300 blooms only a week earlier. The garden, now 18 acres in extent, occupies sloping ground on either side of a stream in the valley bottom, which was dammed in 1969 to create two small lakes, and again downstream in 1982 to create a third lake. Much of the garden has been planted with a world-wide variety of trees and shrubs, reflecting Dr Smart's particular interests. We were shown, for example, flowering specimens of *Parrotia persica* (Caucasus), *Pterocarya stenoptera* (China), *Acacia pravissima* (Australia) *Staphylea pinnata* (Southwest Asia), *Rubus spectabilis* 'Olympic Double' (Canada) and *Skimmia × confusa* 'Kew Green', a notable weeping form of *Cercidiphyllum japonicum*, and a range of trees grown for their ornamental bark (birches and eucalypts, *Acer griseum, Prunus serrula, Myrtus lechleriana* and *Clethra barbinervis,* for example). There are notable collections of *Astilbe, Eucryphia, Iris, Tulbaghia,* and specific areas of the garden are given over to bog plants, North American prairie plants, rock plants, and even an area of mature sessile oak woodland (where purple emperor butterflies, *Apatura iris,* have been seen).

Interspersed among these trees and shrubs we were shown a variety of magnolias (recently featured on BBC *Gardener's World*) and rhododendrons in flower. Magnolias included a range of Jury hybrids from New Zealand ('Apollo', 'Black Tulip', 'Iolanthe' and 'Milky Way'), together with 'Galaxy', 'Heaven Scent', 'Leonard Messel', 'Nimbus', 'Pinkie' and 'Yellow Fever'. Rhododendron species included *R. arboreum, R. basilicum, R. fictolacteum* and *R. niveum;* notable hybrids included 'Alison Johnstone', 'Elizabeth', 'Queen of Hearts', 'Rothenburg', 'Sir Charles Lemon', and a range of *R. davidsonianum* and *R. cinnabarinum* hybrids (including 'Bodnant Yellow' and 'Trewithen Orange'). We saw few camellias in the garden as a whole (a notable hedge of 'Donation'), and by the time we came to the large glasshouse in the walled garden where more than 100 varieties have been growing since 1969, lunch was unfortunately a priority for most members of the party. Fifteen camellias raised at Marwood Hill have received the RHS Award of Merit over the years: 'Annie Wylam', 'Bonnie Marie', 'Carolyn Snowdon', 'Debbie', 'Easter Morn', 'Francie L.', 'Harold Paige', 'Mandalay Queen', 'Margaret Davis', 'Matador', 'Pink Jade', 'Snow Chan', 'Spring Mist', 'Vallee Knudsen' and 'White Nun'.

John Tallis

Gorwell House (22 April 2005)

And so we came to the last garden of the tour, Gorwell House in Barnstaple. The home of Dr John and Mrs Vanessa Marston. It was perhaps a shade of bad luck that the weather had suddenly become much cooler and rain and winds swept over us as we followed John out into his very special garden.

John had one evening earlier in the week, with much humour, presented a recent plant-hunting tour to inner China and continued now in similar fashion, accompanied by botanist friend Martin Rix, with a brisk tour of the garden. First a wander through the walled garden, crammed with exotic and rare plants, many of which were new to some of us.

Among other interesting plants in the garden were twelve different species of palm trees. Moving through the former bullock field, we could enjoy the lovely raised beds filled with plants and numerous shrubs and trees. Among other fine specimens were a tulip tree planted in 1977, magnolias 'Yellow River', 'Wada's Memory', 'Heaven Scent', 'Elizabeth', 'Gold Star', 'Iolanthe', 'Star Wars', × *loebneri* 'Merrill' and a fine *M. delavayi* planted in 1982.

We wandered past manicured yew and thuja hedges, via summerhouses, temples, a shell house, seats and statuary. Many of Vanessa's lovely statues could be seen near the house. Cedars, *Cinnamomum camphora, Eucalyptus nitens,* Kashmir cypress, a *Podocarpus, Liriodendron chinense* (Chinese tulip tree), *Telopea mongaensis,* rhododendrons *R. johnstoneanum,* 'Avalanche', 'Saffron Queen' and 'Winsome', a *Cunninghamia* (Chinese fir), *Davidia involucrata, Euptelea polyandra* with lovely red new growth, *Quercus suber* and much, much more, all carefully guarded by large Monterey pines.

The tour was hurried up a little as we headed indoors to enjoy a warming cup of tea or coffee, which Martin had prepared. We were welcomed by the "hopelessly friendly" family dogs, whom John assured us would wag their tails at any visitor, friend or intruder!

Gorwell House garden is a little bit special, a little different and John obviously has a passion for plants. It is interesting that so many unusual and exotic plants are thriving here. John and Martin were enthusiastically thanked for their efforts and hospitality before we left for Plymouth. John was presented with a *Rhododendron maoerense* AC 4207.

Alan Duncanson

COMPETITIONS

MICHAEL SHUTTLEWORTH

Rhododendron irroratum 'Polka Dot' – winner of Class 10 for Borde Hill Garden

**The Main Rhododendron Show – Species
Borde Hill Garden, Sussex
23–24 April 2005**

This show and competition was sponsored by Loder Plants , Starborough Nurseries and The High Beeches Garden. Following the success of 2004, a marquee of almost twice the size was commissioned for 2005. In spite of dreadful weather in the weeks before the event, with warm spells followed by severe frosts across the South of England, this larger marquee was well filled with outstanding displays of camellias and rhododendrons and a very satisfactory display of magnolias.

It was an especial privilege to welcome a Scottish garden in the presence of the enthusiasts from Dawyck Botanic Garden. On the other hand, it was sad to see that Wakehurst and Leonardslee, both just a few miles away and with outstanding collections of rhododendrons, were absent.

The species exhibits included plenty for the connoisseur of rarities. There was a very nice *R. eudoxum* from Dawyck, *R. spilotum* and *R. vernicosum,* in the shape of the former var. *euanthum,* from Nymans, *R. habrotrichum* F27343 (see picture, next page) from Windsor with subtle colouration of both stem and corolla – an outstanding

99

Rhododendron habrotrichum
F27343 shown by the
Royal Gardens Windsor
in Class 6

MIKE ROBINSON

Glischra species seen far too infrequently. Brian Wright showed us *R. coriaceum* (far too little grown) and Nymans *R. denudatum* C&H 7118, an attractive recent introduction which is becoming better known.

Outstanding, impressive and beautiful were the quite remarkable *R. lanatum* (see picture, opposite) with seven flowers in the truss from Val Fleming, and the *R. hodgsonii* C&H581 from Windsor was perfect in foliage with a good deep pink truss. *R. argyrophyllum* W4276 from Borde Hill was a delicate pink, deeper at the margins and surely worthy of an award. Borde Hill also allowed us to enjoy R. 'Ho Emma' AM (*R. degronianum* subsp. *heptamerum* var. *heptamerum*, formerly *R. metternichii*), which everyone can grow. The truss and spray of *R. pingianum* (see picture, page 102) from Nymans again reminded us that this species has both good foliage – one of the whitest indumenta of the genus and subtly contrasting flowers, which it produces in plenty. *R. cinnabarinum* Sich2470 has flowers of a superb deep reddish pink, and is

excellent even within the delightful flowers of this species, and *R. rarilepidotum* from Chris Fairweather showed that vireyas can be both brightly coloured and subtly beautiful.

Finally what a year for *R. davidsonianum* – diversity in colour and size, unanimity in elegance – a great species!

There were 19 competitors, showing 126 exhibits, with amateurs outnumbering the 'big gardens' by over two to one. The judges noted the extremely high standard in the very demanding classes 1 to 4.

The winners in each class were:

Class 1 (six species), 6 entries: Borde Hill for *R. arboreum, R. argyropyllum, R. falconeri, R. fictolacteum,* and *R. fulvum*

Class 2 (three species), 6 entries: High Beeches for *R. arboreum* var. *roseum, R. fictolacteum* and *R. kesangiae*

Class 3 (one species), 10 entries: Windsor for *R. hodgsonii* C&H581

Class 4 (one species – spray), 10 entries: Nymans for *R. pingianum* Guix125

Class 5 (Arborea, Argyrophylla), 10 entries: Borde Hill for *R. arboreum* subsp. *delavayi*

Class 6 (Barbata, Glischra, Maculifera), 10

entries: Borde Hill for *R. pachysanthum*

Class 7 (Campanulata, Fulgensia, Lanata), 4 entries: Val Fleming for *R. lanatum*

Class 8 (Falconera, Grandia), 7 entries: Mike Robinson for *R. sp. nov.* AC431 Vietnam

Class 9 (Fortunea), 4 entries: Nymans for *R. vernicosum* ('var. *euanthum*')

Class 10 (Irrorata), 5 entries: Borde Hill for *R. irroratum* 'Polka Dot' (see picture, page 99)

Class 11 (Taliensia), 5 entries: Nymans for *R. wightii* (sic)

Class 12 (Neriiflora), 2 entries: Nymans (second. Prize) for *R. neriiflorum*

Class 13 (Pontica), 4 entries: Windsor for *R. metternichii* 'Ho Emma'

Class 14 (Thomsonia, Selensia, Campylocarpa), 5 entries: Nymans for *R. wardii* KW 5736

Class 16 (any other elepidote species), 1 entry: Nymans for *R. venator* KW 6485

Class 17 (Maddenia, Ciliicalyx alliances), 5 entries: Dawyck for *R. johnstoneanum*

Class 18 (Dalhousiae, Megacalyx alliances), 1 entry: Chris Fairweather for *R. horlickianum*

Class 19 (Triflora, Heliolepida), 9 entries: Nymans for *R. davidsonianum*

Class 20 (*R. augustinii*), 3 entries: Nymans

Class 21 (Cinnabarina, Tephropepla, Virgata), 5 entries: Borde Hill for *R. cinnabarinum* Purpurellum Group

Class 23 (Lapponica), 2 entries: High Beeches for *R. hippophaeoides*

Class 24 (Saluenensia, Uniflora), 1 entry: Nymans (Second Prize) for *R. prunifolium*

Class 25 (Scabrifolia), 2 entries: Dawyck (Second Prize) for *R. scabrifolium* var. *spiciferum*

Class 27 (Any other Lepidote species), 1 entry: no award

The outstanding *Rhododendron lanatum*, which won Class 7 for Val Flemming

Class 28 (Vireya), 3 entries: Chris Fairweather for *R. macgregoriae*

Class 29 (Deciduous Azaleas), 5 entries: Nymans for *R. schlippenbachii*

Classes 15, 22, 26 and 30 had no exhibits.

Mike Robinson

The Main Rhododendron Show – Hybrids
23–24 April 2005

The 30 hybrid classes were supported by 14 gardens that, between them, displayed 128 vases brimming with colour and interest, if not always beauty.

Exbury again won more first prizes than anyone else and regained The Crosfield Challenge Cup (for three hybrids bred and raised in the exhibitor's garden) that they lost last April for the first time in years. But in spite of Exbury's well-deserved prominence, they didn't dominate the Hybrids Section. Indeed, they won fewer prizes overall than either Barry Haseltine or Brian Wright who, in Sussex, both garden on infinitely smaller

The truss of *Rhododendron pingianum* Guix125, which won Class 4 for Nymans Garden

MIKE ROBINSON

patches; so does size matter after all? Usually it does, but for the moment let's dwell a little less on rivalry and more on some of the blooms which helped to make this year's Competition the undoubted attraction that it was.

The opening class was for six hybrid trusses. It attracted three entrants all of whom mustered some fine exhibits. Exbury produced 'Aurora', 'Diane', 'Gaul', 'Lionel's Triumph', 'Pearl Betteridge' and 'Queen of Hearts' – a group of now famous hybrids which was awarded first prize. Second prize was won by Ann Hooton with 'Caroline de Zoete', a pretty pink tinged white *R. williamsianum* cross made by Hydon Nurseries, 'Cornish Cross', 'Mariloo Gilbury', the star-rated, pale creamy pink Exbury clone, 'Quaker Girl', 'Queen of Hearts' and the brilliant red 'Taurus'. Third prize went to The Crown Estate Commissioners, Windsor for big, bold heads of 'Beatrice Keir' (a rather striking chartreuse green) 'Lamellen', 'Pink Bride' and 'Pink Glory' (two typical early Loder crosses) and 'Red Glow'.

The class for three trusses was won by The National Trust Garden of Nymans. They showed a well presented trio of 'Blewbury' (that good *roxieanum* hybrid) 'Taurus' and 'Unique'. Very close, in second place, came High Beeches with an all-white entry viz. 'Elsae' (the impressive *R. grande/hodgsonii* cross), 'Two Kings' (see picture, opposite) (no prizes for guessing which Kings) and a clone from the 'White Glory' grex. Third prize went to Brian Wright for 'Robert Keir' (a *R. lacteum* cross by J.B. Stevenson), 'Sir Charles Lemon' and 'Unique'. With seven entrants, all quite close, Exbury were awarded a fourth prize for a notable big-leaved entry of 'Colonel Rogers' (see picture, page 104), 'Fortune' and an unnamed *R. hodgsonii* cross.

The Loder Cup class requiring just one truss from each entrant brought a fierce challenge from 16 competitors making it the best supported class in the Competition. The trophy went to Ann Hooton who staged a superb vase of 'Taurus' – 'Jean Marie de Montague' × *R. strigillosum*. This was indeed a worthy winner: a tight round truss of

Orient red, campanulate flowers poised on a skirt of deep green lance-like leaves. The runners-up were Brian Wright with 'Robert Keir' and Borde Hill with that old Dutch Master, 'Boddaertianum'.

Exbury won the first of the spray classes with a stunning offering of 'St Tudy'. This *R. impeditum/augustinii* cross may be described as lobelia blue but on the Borde Hill showbench it was electric. But quite as good in second place was Nymans' 'Yellow Hammer'. At one time at Vincent Square there was a class exclusively for this *R. sulfureum × flavidum* hybrid. Nowadays, it's not so much seen. Nevertheless, this exhibit, packed with deep yellow flowers, was the best 'Yellow Hammer' I had seen for some time. In third place came High Beeches with a mammoth branch of 'White Glory'. Very grand but not nearly as fetching as its dwarfer opposition.

As mentioned earlier, Exbury regained The Crosfield Cup. Their three winning trusses were an unnamed cross of *R. eclecteum* and 'Avalanche', hodgsonii hybrid 'Halton' (a clone of the 'Lionel's Triumph' grex), which was at one time described as being the species but later considered to be of hybrid origin by Davidian, and 'Queen of Hearts'. This was a magnificent entry showing the Exbury hybrids, at least at this event, at their very best.

In over 25 years of show reporting, I cannot recall an empty Loderi Group class. This year it happened. No Loderis! Whatever next?

The class for subsection Grandia and Falconera hybrids was interesting. It produced a first prize for High Beeches who showed the fine home-raised 'Little Jessica'. Second prize went to Exbury for their

Rhododendron 'Two Kings' – a Loderi cross from the High Beeches

renowned 'Fortune' and third to Dr Mike Robinson for a good but unnamed entry. This class also produced an intriguing truss labelled 'Colonel Rogers'. Almost lilac and therefore much paler than the typical mauve of the well-known deliberate hybrid, this was said to be a natural hybrid from the same parents i.e. *R. falconeri* and *R. niveum*. The entry came from the granddaughter of *the* Colonel Rogers, a great rhododendron enthusiast who, I understand, spent some time in Sikkim and Bhutan where *R. falconeri* and *R. niveum* both occur.

Hybrids, with more regularity than they should, appear in the species classes. It is not often the other way about but this year *R. bureavii* 'Lem's Favorite' broke the mould. That is, it did if you ignore some expert opinion which sees the plant as a hybrid. Anyhow, it appeared first as a truss in the class for exhibits with subsection Taliensia parentage and then in the class for exhibits with

Rhododendron 'Colonel Rogers' (left) (*niveum × falconeri*) a truss of the original plant, possibly a natural hybrid from Sikkim, with alongside (right) the more normal deeper shade of the deliberate cross entered by Exbury

subsection Pontica parentage; since it could be argued that *R. bureavii* 'Lem's Favorite' also possesses *R. yakushimanum* blood. The outcome was that the exhibit was awarded first prizes in both classes. So, as far as its owner Brian Wright was concerned, nothing was lost.

John Lancaster of Balcombe Forest in West Sussex should be congratulated on the spray of 'Alison Johnstone' he entered in the class for exhibits with Cinnabarina parentage. This displayed a most generous amount of pale amber/pink flowers set off by blue/green waxy leaves. An altogether beautiful vase which deservedly won first prize.

In the class for exhibits grown under glass, Chris Fairweather provided a show of his own by entering eight vireyas. Prizes went to 'Halo' (first), a dream in shades of vermilion, orange and peach; 'Shantung Pearl' (second); and 'Just Peachy' (third), a kind of satiny yellow apricot. There was also an unplaced exhibit showing long, horn-like flowers of apricot – a sort of lavish HMV logo. It was called 'Bold Janus'.

In the classes for competitors with gardens under three acres, Barry Haseltine did well by winning six of the nine awarded prizes. His best, I thought, were the species *R. morii* (quite white) the enchanting Exbury hybrid 'Carita' and the unfamiliar 'April Snow' with its somewhat bi-generic look. In this section, top prizes also went to John Rawling with his more rose-flushed *R. morii* and John Lancaster for his promiscuous but very good *R. primuliflorum*.

The trade stands offered an out-of-the-ordinary range of plants of particular interest to enthusiasts: Coghurst Camellias (camellias), Witch Hazel Nursery (magnolias), Ian Fitzroy (acers), Loder Plants (rhododendrons) and Chris Fairweather (vireyas).

Brian Wright

Early Camellia Competition
15 March 2005

A week or so before the event, we saw temperatures plummet to −9°C, 6m camellia trees weighted almost to the ground with snow and snowmen who resided with us for almost a week. This polar scene, experienced in Crowborough, East Sussex, was repeated to a greater or lesser degree in various parts of the country. It was no wonder then that those who had the protection of glass could really make a fist of showing at the Early Camellia Competition held at Vincent Square. Indeed, the stats speak for themselves:

In the Bloom, as opposed to the Spray, classes, 51 first, second and third prizes were awarded. Of these, 37 went to entries grown under glass while only two blooms grown in the open succeeded in winning first prizes against glass-grown opposition.

As things stood, Chatsworth House Trust came top of the glass with a haul of 24 first, second and third prizes, 10 of which were 'firsts'. Behind them, and at the other end of the gardening scale with only a 12ft × 6ft greenhouse and four 'hi-jacked' parking spaces, came Alan Smith of Swanage (alkaline country). He achieved seven prizes, five of them 'firsts'. Outstanding among these pot-grown successes were: 'Lovelight' (see picture, above), a voluptuous semi-double white *C. japonica* introduced by the Californian grower Harvey Short; 'Margaret Davis', that delectable, internationally accoladed double *C. japonica* – a ruffled ivory posy edged in deep lilac pink; 'Mirage', a bright rose-red semi-double *C.* × *williamsii* with a boss of striking yellow anthers; 'Anticipation', the popular purple-pink paeony-formed *C.* × *williamsii* created by Les

Camellia japonica 'Lovelight' – a prize-winning bloom entered in the Early Camellia Competition by Alan Smith of Swanage.

Jury and, in this case, impressively grown by Alan Smith.

Of particular note from Chatsworth were 'Easter Morn', 'Kramer's Beauty', 'Guest of Honour', 'Drama Girl', 'Guilio Nuccio' and 'R.L. Wheeler'. It was this all-American collection that won first prize in the Six Japonica class. All were outstandingly large blooms (some as hefty as the big reticulatas) and all raised in California, apart from 'R.L. Wheeler', which was Georgia born.

Chatsworth also won four out of the six classes which called for three blooms, and well-remembered here were the trio that topped the class for anemone and paeony formed japonicas; these were the dark red 'Dixie Knight', the old but still elegant 'Elegans' and the suggestively fringed 'Hawaii'. There was also a good 'Captain Rawes', the first *C. reticulata* ever to reach these shores from China 185 years ago. Many competitions earlier, I cheekily, and somewhat ignorantly, asked Chatsworth's then head gardener if he would kindly graft one for me. Now, with a little more camellia experience, I know why he didn't take up the challenge. However, this year's 'Captain' deservedly won first prize in the *C. reticulata* class. In the same class, Chatsworth also did well with a fine 'Francie L.' It was given third prize even though it should have been shown in the class that called for any retic crossed with a *C.* × *williamsii* or *C. saluenensis* variety; 'Francie L's parentage being *C. reticulata* 'Buddha' (which involves *C. pitardii*) × *saluenensis* 'Apple Blossom'.

Along with other competitors who showed impressive blooms was David Davis. He was a marginally close runner-up to Chatsworth in the 'any six' japonicas class. His entry, which comprised 'Margaret Davis' (no relation) 'Elegans Champagne', 'Vulcan', 'Twilight', 'Nuccio's Pearl' and 'Shiro Chan', had been carefully selected from some very well-grown plants – an exhibit indeed of high quality. His third placed entry in the three japonicas class, was again virtually faultless except that his chosen three viz. 'Nuccio's Pearl' (exquisite), 'Twilight' and 'Vulcan' had already appeared in the 'any six' class, which, by the rules received by every competitor, made them ineligible. This is the second year in a row that David has advantageously contravened this regulation and, of course, the second consecutive year that both the stewards and judges have failed to spot the offence. Regrettably, one can only say, "Do wake up chaps!" Nothing was amiss, however, in the class for any formal double japonica which David Davis won with his irresistible 'Nuccio's Pearl'.

Of those entries grown outside, Mrs Griffiths (Thames Ditton), Mrs Keates (Kingston-on-Thames), and Jill Totty (Fordingbridge, Hants) did as well as they could against glass-protected opposition.

Mrs Griffiths picked-up prizes in five classes with her best effort being in the class for three *C.* × *williamsii* blooms. Here, she got the better of Chatsworth with a first prize for 'J.C. Williams', 'Mary Christian' and 'Blue Danube'.

There were also prizes in five classes for Mrs Keates who too overcame Chatsworth to gain first prize for her 'Jury's Yellow' in the 'yellow' cultivar class. On the other hand, she was very hard done by when her excellent 'Desire' (a camellia worthy of any collection) was given only a miserly fourth prize in the class for rose-formed japonicas.

Jill Totty did not manage a first prize but showed some charming miniatures in the class for three anemone/paeony formed cultivars. These were 'Tinker Toy', a creamy white flecked in red, and the popular reds 'Bob's Tinsie' and 'Little Bit'; well-worth the second prize they received. And well-worth their third prize were those she entered in the 'any six' class viz. 'Bob's Tinsie', 'Mark Alan' (a beautiful claret colour with spoon-shaped petaloids interspersed with bright yellow stamens), 'Ruddigore', 'Adolphe Audusson', 'Margaret Davis' and 'Spencer's Pink'.

Possibly Andy Simons was the only competitor to enter blooms grown both in the open and under glass. His efforts were rewarded with first, second and third prizes in the species class and prizes in four other classes. His species were *C. saluenensis* and *C. forrestii* from Yunnan and *C. transnokoensis* from Taiwan. He also won a first for 'Quintessence', the very pretty trailing patio plant that is a cross between a *C. japonica* seedling and *C. lutchuensis*.

Brian Wright

Main Camellia Show
12–13th April 2005

Just when we thought that showing couldn't get much better for David Davis, it did. For a record fourth year in a row he won The Leonardslee Bowl for the Show's best exhibit of twelve blooms. This feat has been matched only once before by Mrs C. Petherick from 1989 to 1992. Two others viz. Sir Giles Loder and Mrs. P. Eunson have achieved a commendable hat-trick of wins but only the former pair has lifted the trophy four times running. For those who would love to know the secret of such consistently good growing and showing, you would need to ask David Davis, although I can reveal that his winning dozen this year were the japonicas 'Annie Wylam', 'Bob Hope', 'Elegans Champagne', 'Guilio Nuccio', 'Kitty Berry', 'Midnight Magic', 'Shiro Chan', 'Swan Lake' (see picture, opposite) and 'Tiffany'; the *C. reticulata* hybrids 'Lasca Beauty' and 'Tom Knudson'; the *C. × williamsii* 'Wilber Foss'.

Behind this entry came that of Andy Simons who must also be heartily congratulated. Not only was Andy's twelve almost inseparably close to the winner's but he backed this with a further entry that was placed third. So Andy gave us 24 different and altogether superb blooms to enjoy. These were, in second place, the japonicas 'Augusto Pinto', 'Easter Morn', 'Kramer's Supreme', 'Nuccio's Cameo', 'Nuccio's Gem', 'R.L. Wheeler' and 'Spring Formal'; the *C. reticulata* hybrids 'Hulyn Smith', 'Jean Pursel', 'Raspberry Glow' and 'Valentine Day'; the *C. pitardii* hybrid 'Peggy Burton'. In third place, the japonicas 'Kramer's Beauty', 'Lily Pons', 'Mark Alan', 'Nuccio's Carousel', 'Owen Henry', 'White Nun' and

Camellia japonica 'Swan Lake' – one of David Davis' prize-winning entries at the Main Camellia Show at Westminster on 12th April 2005

MICHEAL SHUTTLEWORTH

'William Honey'; the *C. reticulata* hybrids 'Bravo', 'Chrissie's Retic', 'Lasca Beauty' and 'Pearl Terry' plus an unknown bloom.

In all, eleven entries totalling 132 top quality blooms contested the coveted Leonardslee Bowl. Tough for the challengers but a feast of flower for the public.

Overall, the event itself broke-down into 24 classes: 18 for blooms, 5 for sprays and 1 for a free arrangement of camellias. This schedule attracted 159 entries which resulted in a stunning display of well over 400 flowers.

Prize-wise, David Davis collected more first prizes than any other competitor – six in all. Andy Simons bagged most prizes overall with eighteen first, second and third prizes while there were fine efforts from Ann Hooton (13 prizes) and Nick Creek (10 prizes).

Controversy still persists over the RHS Shows Department's insistence on judging entries grown in the open alongside those grown under protection. The objection,

MICHEAL SHUTTLEWORTH

An unnamed *Camellia cuspidata* hybrid exhibited at the Main Camellia Competition

mainly from those growing in the open, is understandable since growing under glass or plastic is not merely just about protection and thus better quality blooms, it's about a totally different type of growing to enhance bloom size and quality. Very often plants grown in a protected environment receive individual care, involving skilful disbudding, bud selection and isolation plus planned feeding procedures. Such husbandry rarely takes place with plants grown in the open which means that competition between protected and unprotected plants is largely unequal. Moreover, the position – in spite of the differentiating red spot, which is often not understood – is misleading for the viewing public. This is to say, that, apart from the alpine and daffodil competitions, more plant wish lists are compiled on the camellia show benches than anywhere else in the Vincent Square halls. If, therefore, it is not understood that blooms grown under cover may be quite different in size, form, colour and quality from their outside-grown

counterparts, there could be many disappointed gardening enthusiasts whose camellia purchases, when grown in the open, do not come up to expectations. All this may not cut much ice with the RHS who are, after all, primarily interested in having on show the best specimens they can. But food for thought is the fact that some exhibitors, who have been supporting the camellia competitions for 20 or 30 years, are finally so unhappy with matters that they are considering abandoning the Westminster camellia shows altogether. If they do, then the shows could be weakened for the sake of some fairly straightforward adjustments by the RHS Shows Department.

Elsewhere, David toppled Goliath in the 'any six' cultivar class. David (Andy Simons) showed five japonicas viz. 'Ave Maria', 'Black Tie', 'Takanini', 'Tom Thumb' and 'Wilamina' plus the *C. × williamsii × japonica* 'Black Opal'. All were grown outside apart from 'Black Opal' and all, compared to the Goliath proportions of Alan Smith's (the runner-up) entry, were comparative miniatures. Alan showed a grown-under-glass, larger-than-life sextet of the japonicas 'Bob Hope', 'Dixie Knight', 'Grand Prix', 'Jupiter' and 'Lovelight' plus the popular *C. × williamsii* 'Anticipation'. These blooms were not only spectacularly big but inevitably pristine. Trouble was, they could not match the winner's smaller flowers in the charm department. In the wake of these entries, in third place, came a most creditable selection of open-grown blooms from Mrs Ann Hooton. She gave us the japonicas 'Betty Sheffield Supreme', the fine white 'Joshua E. Youtz', 'Mattie Cole' and 'Miss Charleston' along with the *C. × williamsii* hybrids 'Anticipation' and the delectable 'Dream Boat'.

In the *C. japonica* classes, those entries grown in the open actually held their own against those grown under glass by winning half of the first, second and third prizes awarded. Outstanding among these were singles from Nick Creek who won the 'three' class with 'Evelyn', 'Furo-an' and 'Mattie Cole' and the 'one' class with the impressive 'Clarissa'. Also of some merit were Jill Totty's dark reds: 'Grand Slam', 'San Dimas' and 'Bob Hope', which came second in the semi-double class for three blooms. But the best of the japonicas were those exhibited by David Davis. He gave us six stunning flowers – plump and perfect – which took two first prizes; one for three anemone-formed blooms ('Swan Lake', 'Tiffany' and 'Elegans Champagne') the other for three formal double blooms ('Berenice Perfection', 'Opal Princess' and 'Nuccio's Pearl'). If you are able to grow under glass and as well as David Davis does, then put any of these camellias on your shopping list and you'll have years of gardening pleasure.

In the remaining classes, the reticulatas took centre stage. Their specific class was not only outstanding in colour, form and size but attracted more entries than any other class in the competition – and this at a time when there are frequent appeals for this species and its hybrids to be more widely grown. Anyway, the outcome was first prize for 'Lasca Beauty', that highly impressive soft pink, semi-double created by Dr Clifford Parks and shown on this occasion by David Davis. In second place was the rather sensational 'Raspberry Glow' from Andy Simons. For a chance, second generation seedling from the far more ancient 'Crimson Robe', this plant produces a remarkable crimson flower with a light base which really does make it glow. Third place was given to

MICHEAL SHUTTLEWORTH

Magnolia 'Lois' – Maurice Foster's Best in Show winner in the Southeast Branch Magnolia Competition

Mrs Ann Hooton's 'Royalty', a big, bright red semi-double with a striking cluster of yellow stamens.

The *C. × williamsii* classes always produce some very tastefully shaped flowers, often precise and symmetrically pleasing. This year was no exception with 'Elizabeth Anderson' and 'E.G. Waterhouse' coming from Jill Totty, 'Water Lily' from Nick Creek and 'Rose Parade' from Ann Hooton – all noteworthy prize-winners. Mention must also made of 'Les Jury', the fabulous red that gained a first prize for Ann Hooton in the formal double class.

In the spray classes it was Ann Hooton who kept the show on the road. She entered at least nine vases in four classes and collected some well-won prizes.

Brian Wright

Southeast Branch Magnolia Competition

The magnolia classes filled a whole wall of the marquee, and made a beautiful and impressive tribute to this wonderful genus: it was a pleasant surprise to see so many entries after the poor weather, demonstrating what can be done when the flowers do not have to travel hundreds of miles before being placed on the show bench.

There were 44 exhibits in 9 classes from 9 exhibitors. Maurice Foster took the cup for the highest cumulative score, and Barry Haseltine the cup for the best exhibitor with a garden of under 3 acres.

Interesting exhibits were the new 'Felix Jury' from Mike Robinson, a very nice spray of 'Caerhays Belle' from Maurice, and no fewer than three exhibits of 'Dianica' (*Michelia yunnanensis*), two of which had been grown outside, but the *pièce de resistance* was 'Lois' (see picture, previous page), which has the most outstandingly elegant form and a true daffodil yellow colour. Naturally it won best in show – by a mile.

Mike Robinson

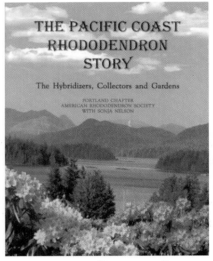

RHS Rhododendron and Camellia Committee

Chairman
J G Hillier, c/o Hillier Nurseries, Ampfield House, Ampfield, Romsey, Hants SO51 9PA

Vice-Chairman
J T Gallagher, Oldfield, 29 Moorlands Road, Verwood, Dorset BH31 6PD

Secretary
Dr N Lancaster, RHS Garden Wisley, Woking, Surrey GU23 6QB

Members
Lady Aberconway, 25 Egerton Terrace, London SW3 2DP
The Hon. Edward Boscawen, The Garden House, High Beeches Lane, Handcross, Sussex RH17 6HQ
C Fairweather, Beacon Gate, Beaulieu, Hampshire SO42 7YR
M Flanagan, Verderers, Wick Road, Englefield Green, Egham, Surrey TW20 3AE
M C Foster, White House Farm, Ivy Hatch, Sevenoaks, Kent TN15 0NN
A F George, Hydon Nurseries, Hydon Heath, Godalming, Surrey GU8 4AZ
Dr R H L Jack, Edgemoor, Loch Road, Lanark ML11 9BG
D G Millais, Crosswater Farm, Churt, Farnham, Surrey GU10 2JN
M Pharoah, Marwood Hill, Marwood, Barnstaple, Devon EX31 4EB
Dr M L A Robinson, Hindhead Lodge, Priory Road, Forest Row, E Sussex RH18 5JF
A W Simons, Wingfield House, 11 Brinsmade Road, Ampthill, Bedfordshire
A V Skinner, MBE, 2 Frog Firle Cottage, Alfriston, nr Polegate, E Sussex BN26 5TT
M O Slocock, VMH, Knap Hill Nursery, Barrs Lane, Knaphill, Woking, Surrey GU21 2JW
C B Tomlin, Starborough Nursery, Starborough Road, Marsh Green, Edenbridge, Kent TN8 5RB
Miss J Trehane, 353 Church Cottages, Hampreston, Wimborne, Dorset BH21 7LX
C H Williams, Burncoose Nurseries, Gwennap, Redruth, Cornwall TR16 6BJ
F J Williams, Caerhays Castle, Gorran, St Austell, Cornwall PL26 6LY

Horticultural Board Representative
C P Ellis, 39 West Square, London SE11 4SP

RHS Rhododendron, Camellia and Magnolia Group

---❦---

Officers

Chairman Dr M L A ROBINSON, Hindleap Lodge, Priory Road, Forest Row, E Sussex
RH18 5JF (Tel: 01342 822745, Email: mlarob@hotmail.com)

Hon. Treasurer Mr Martin D C GATES, 12 Marlborough Road, Chandlers Ford,
Eastleigh, Hants SO53 5DH (Tel: 023 8025 2843)

Hon. Secretary Mrs Pat BUCKNELL, Botallick, Lanreath, Looe, Cornwall PL13 2PF (Tel:
01503 220215, Email: PatBucknell@tiscali.co.uk)

Hon. Membership Secretary Mr Rupert L C ELEY, East Bergholt Place, East Bergholt,
Suffolk CO7 6UP (Tel: 01206 298385, Fax: 01206 299224,
Email: sales@placeforplants.co.uk)

Hon. Yearbook Editor Mr Philip D EVANS, West Netherton, Drewsteignton, Devon
EX6 6RB (Tel/fax: 01647 281285, Email: philip.d.evans@talk21.com)

Hon. Bulletin Editor Mr John A RAWLING, The Spinney, Station Road, Woldingham,
Surrey CR3 7DD (Tel: 01883 653341, Email: jr.eye@virgin.net)

Hon. Tours Organiser Vacancy

Webmaster Mr Graham MILLS, Tregoning Mill, St Kevern, Helston, Cornwall TR12 6QE
(Email: graham@tregoningmill.co.uk)

Committee Members

Mr Maurice C FOSTER, White House Farm, Ivy Hatch, Sevenoaks, Kent TN15 0NN
(Tel: 01732 810634, Fax: 01732 810553, Email: RosieFoster@aol.com)

Mr John D HARSANT, Newton House, Wall Lane, Heswell, Wirral, Merseyside L60 8NF
(Tel: 0151 342 3664, Fax: 0151 348 4015, email: john@harsant.uk.com)

Dr R H L JACK, Edgemoor, Loch Road, Lanark ML11 9BG (Tel: 01555 663021)

Mr Alastair T STEVENSON, Appledore, Upton Bishop, Ross-on-Wye,
Herefordshire HR9 7UL (Tel: 01989 780285, Fax: 01989 780591,
email: alastairstevenson@tiscali.co.uk (Co-ordinator of Events and Publicity Officer)

Mr Ivor T STOKES, Llyshendy, Llandeilo, Carmarthenshire SA19 6YA (Tel/fax: 01558
823233, email: ivor.stokes@btopenworld.com)

Mr Brian E WRIGHT, Kilsaren, Fielden Lane, Crowborough, Sussex TN6 1TL (Tel:
01892 653207, Fax: 01892 669550, Email: iriswright@msn.com)

Branch Chairmen

International vacancy

New Forest Mr Christopher FAIRWEATHER, The Garden Centre, High Street, Beaulieu, Hants
SO42 7YR (Tel: 01590 612307, Fax: 01590 612519, email: chrisfairweather@waitrose.com)

Norfolk Vacancy

North Wales and Northwest Mr C E J BRABIN, Rosewood, Puddington Village, Neston
   CH64 5SS (Tel: 0151 353 1193)
Peak District Dr David R IVES, 18 Park Road, Birstall, Leicestershire LE4 3AU (Tel: 0116
   2675118, Email: rosidavid.ives@btopenworld.com)
Southeast Mr Barry HASELTINE, Goodwins, Snow Hill, Crawley Down, Sussex
   RH10 3EF (Tel: 01342 713132, Email: barry.haseltine@which.net)
Southwest Dr Alun J B EDWARDS, Spinney, Park Lane, Barnstaple, Devon EX32 9AJ
   (Tel: 01271 343324, email: alun.edwards@which.net)
Ulster Mr Patrick FORDE, Seaforde, Downpatrick, Co Down BT30 8PG
   (Tel: 01396 811225, Fax: 01396 811370, Email: Plants@SeafordeGardens.com)
Wessex Mrs Miranda GUNN, Ramster, Petworth Road, Chiddingfold, Surrey GU8 4SN
   (Tel: 01428 644422, Fax: 01428 658345, email: Ramsterweddings@tiscali.co.uk)
Convenor of Group Seed Bank Mr Henry (Chip) LIMA, 11 Robert Bruce Court, Larbert,
   Stirlingshire, Scotland FK5 4HP
   (Tel: 01324 552169, Email: vireyachip@btinternet.com)
Advertising Mr Brian E WRIGHT, Kilsaren, Fielden Lane, Crowborough, Sussex TN6 1TL
   (Tel: 01892 653207, Fax: 01892 669550, Email: iriswright@msn.com)
Yearbook Archivist Mrs Pam HAYWARD, Woodtown, Sampford Spiney, Yelverton, Devon
   PL20 6LJ (Tel/fax: 01822 852122, Email: WoodtownPam@aol.com)

Membership: for details of Membership please contact the Hon. Membership Secretary
Website addresses: rhodogroup-rhs.org   magnoliasociety.org   vireya.net

Dunge Valley Hidden Gardens

2006 will be our best flowering season ever.

The gardens at 1,000 feet in the Pennine hills are a real pleasure both to the discerning rhododendron enthusiast or the casual visitor with a huge range of hybrids and species complemented by a collection of rare trees and shrubs.

PLANT SALE

We are having a clear out of our rare trees, rhododendrons and magnolias. There is a vast choice available from wild-collected *Rhododendron* species such as *R. falconeri* subsp *eximium, R. hookerii, R. flinkii, R. bhutanense, R. edgeworthii* and *R. griffithianum;* in fact some 30 plus species, some of which still need naming, from three treks in Arunachal Pradesh in 2003 plus many from treks in Nepal over the last fifteen years.

We also have a large stock of hybrid rhododendrons including about 40 extra large plants at just £35.00 each. Our entire stocks of trees including wild-collected birch, sorbus, etc are being planted out here, but if you want some there are a few left including many named forms.

We still have a lot of magnolias such as 'Star Wars', 'Vulcan', *M. tripetala,* 'Sunburst', *M. campbellii* 'Charles Raffle', etc, which are also are being cleared out!

Open 10-30am 5-00pm.
March and April; June to August: Open Thursday, Friday, Saturday and Sunday.
May: Open every day except Monday.
Always open Bank Holiday Mondays.
Open by appointment in the winter.

SORRY NO MAIL ORDER

A visit to the gardens or nursery is always worthwhile.

Online catalogue: **www.dungevalley.co.uk**
Email: **david@dungevalley.co.uk**
Dunge Valley Hidden Gardens and Hardy Plant Nursery
Windgather Rocks, Kettleshulme, High Peak, Cheshire SK23 7RF
Phone/Fax: **01663 733787**

Index

Australian Rhododendron Society Inc.
www.ausrhodo.asn.au

Overseas members are welcomed – annual dues of $A25.00 (payable by $A bank draft, Visa or Mastercard) cover family membership inclusive of the annual Journal "The Rhododendron" airmailed with news from the Southern Hemisphere of new hybrids, azaleas and Vireyas, and admission to Society gardens in Australia. Subscription year commences 1st July. Membership applications to:

THE SECRETARY,
AUSTRALIAN RHODODENDRON SOCIETY
10 Wilpena Terrace, Aldgate
South Australia 5154

MILLAIS NURSERIES

SPECIALIST GROWERS OF RHODODENDRONS AND AZALEAS

We grow one of the finest ranges of rhododendrons and azaleas in the country.
Come and visit our well-stocked Plant Centre and 10 acres of display gardens
featuring new varieties and old favourites.
Experienced plantsmen to help with your selection.
Acclaimed mail-order service throughout Europe from November to March.

SEE OUR NEW RANGE OF MAGNOLIAS AND ACERS

Our extensive range of rhododendrons includes hardy hybrids, yakushimanums,
dwarf varieties, deciduous and evergreen azaleas, rare species and maddenias.
Everything from historic old cultivars to the latest introductions from America
and Germany. Newly collected species, scented and late-flowering varieties.

Open Monday to Friday 10am–1pm, 2–5pm
Also Saturdays in spring and autumn. Daily in May and early June.

Crosswater Farm, Crosswater Lane, Churt, Farnham, Surrey GU10 2JN
Tel: (01252) 792698   Fax: (01252) 792526

sales@rhododendrons.co.uk   **www.rhododendrons.co.uk**

Glendoick
gardens ltd

Write, phone, fax or e mail for our 70 Page full colour catalogue, or specimen plant list.
Glendoick Gardens, Perth PH2 7NS,

A few of the new Rhododendrons available this year.

R. kasoense a fine Autumn-flowering species introduced for the first time by Peter & Kenneth Cox from Arunachal Pradesh. Reaches 2m in height and should be hardy in most of the UK. Needs good drainage. Also *R. monanthum*, lower growing

'Wine & Roses': this sensational dwarf has masses of pink flowers in May but is chiefly recommended for its dark red leave underside. This is a huge improvement on Rosevallon, looks good year round, and is certain to become a best seller.

'Plover' the latest of the Cox bird hybrids is the first scented pink dwarf we have bred. This hybrid of *R. edgeworthii x R. dendrocharis* is a tidy plant with fine dark foliage and very good deep pink, scented flowers in late April.

New azaleas include the very late scented pale yellow **'Lemon Drop'**, the blue-green leaved **'Baltic Amber'** and the new German yellow **'Gold Topas'** with deep purple young growth.

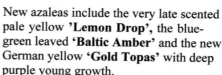

We also stock a fine range of *Kalmia latifolia, Lilium, new Sorbus selections, Chilean plants, Eucryphia, Enkianthus, Trillium, Nomocharis etc*

You can order on line on our web site: www.glendoick.com

A Technicolour Dream

Exbury remains a family garden still full of spirit and enthusiasm for rhododendrons. Mr Edmund de Rothschild warmly welcomes visitors to the Gardens to share the incredible legacy left by his father, Lionel de Rothschild.

Lionel carved Exbury Gardens out of mature New Forest oak woodland during the 1920s and 30s. Today you can enjoy a slice of rhododendron history by admiring his now mature, careful selections and hybrids.

With the Rothschild Collection of Rhododendrons, Azaleas and Camellias – over 200 acres to explore, and the new Steam Railway – you are assured of a colourful day out!

Plant Centre, Gift Shop and Mr Eddy's Restaurant (can all be visited without entering the Gardens). Buggy rides available daily. "Meet and Greet" and tailored talks on any aspect of the Gardens can be arranged on request.

Open daily from 1st March to 5th November 2006. Limited winter opening.

EXBURY
—— GARDENS ——
STEAM RAILWAY

General enquiries: (023) 8089 1203, 24hr info line: (023) 8089 9422 or Plant Centre: (023) 8089 8625

www.exbury.co.uk or email: nigel.philpott@exbury.co.uk

Exbury Gardens, Exbury in the New Forest, near Beaulieu 20 mins drive south from M27 West, Junction 2

Visit in April and May to receive FREE return visit in October!